WARRIOR

To, Robert Brown MSP

Best Wishes

Ian Hamilton

Tam Henderson joined the Black Watch in 1983. Deployed to conflicts in Northern Ireland, the Balkans and the Middle East, he rose through the ranks to captain. He was the youngest quartermaster in the British Army at his time of service and the youngest QM in Iraq in 2005.

As a writer, John Hunt has covered world events such as the end of apartheid, conflicts in Kashmir and Colombia, and the election of Bolivia's first indigenous president. With Ruth Devlin, who edited this book, he is co-founder of the writing agency VividAgenda.com.

WARRIOR

A True Story of Bravery
and Betrayal in the Iraq War

Captain Tam Henderson QM
and John Hunt

MAINSTREAM
PUBLISHING

EDINBURGH AND LONDON

First published in Great Britain in 2008 by
MAINSTREAM PUBLISHING COMPANY
(EDINBURGH) LTD
7 Albany Street
Edinburgh EH1 3UG

ISBN 9781845963965

This book is a work of non-fiction based on the life, experiences
and recollections of Tam Henderson. In some instances, names of people,
places, dates, sequences or the detail of events have been changed to
protect the privacy of others. The authors have stated to the publishers
that, except in such respects, not affecting the substantial
accuracy of the work, the contents of this book are true.

A catalogue record for this book is available
from the British Library

Typeset in Caslon and Century Gothic

Printed in Great Britain by
CPI Mackays of Chatham Ltd, Chatham, ME5 8TD

CONTENTS

Foreword
by Warren Lister

During my long career in engineering, I have dealt with many matters, in and out of courts around the world, involving mixes of technical and human failings. A good few cases have been more convoluted and stranger than fiction and would perhaps make fascinating reading. However, the case of Warrant Officer Thomas Henderson's fight to clear his name and rescue his career deserves special attention, because not only does it show all that is best about the British soldier, it also goes to the heart of Britain's capability to arm itself effectively and defend itself with honour against a troubled world. I commend his story to you, the reader.

Tam Henderson of the Black Watch served at the leading edge of the British Army's advance in the Iraq War. Suffering from a lack of equipment and spares, on 22 March 2003 he and his company commander led C Company into battle at Az Zubayr to take a strategically important barracks. The chain gun on their Warrior failed them again and again, and they only survived by the skin of their teeth. As they returned to their base camp on the night of 24 March, after a dangerous foray to recover the body of Lance Corporal Barry Stephen, whom they had believed might have been alive and in the hands of the Iraqi army, the chain gun fired without warning, injuring Sergeant Albert Thomson, who lost a leg as a result. Tam Henderson was promptly charged and convicted of firing the gun negligently and was removed from his regiment in disgrace.

Tam always maintained that the vehicle and the gun were faulty, that he was innocent of any wrongdoing and that he had been a convenient scapegoat to cover up the MoD's failure to provide safe weapons. It took a year, a detailed independent investigation and a full appeal hearing to clear his name and quash the conviction. I had the privilege of investigating and presenting the technical facts to the military appeal tribunal.

The story of Tam's twenty-four-year career in the army makes fascinating reading. He led from the front in four major campaigns, in Northern Ireland, Kosovo, Macedonia and Iraq. His dedication and courage typify the commitment and professionalism of Britain's great regiments, of which the Black Watch was certainly one. Albert Thomson, Tam Henderson and their comrades in arms deserved better from the MoD.

EurIng Warren Lister CEng,
FIMechE, MIET, MAE, MEWI

June 2008

List of Abbreviations

1MEF	1st Marine Expeditionary Force (US Army)
AAS	armament armed switch (supplies power to the weapons on the Warrior)
AFV	armoured fighting vehicle
ASS	armed selector switch (used to select the chain gun or the Rarden cannon on the Warrior)
BATUK	British Army Training Unit Kenya
BATUS	British Army Training Unit Suffield (in Canada)
CO	Commanding Officer
CONCO	continuity NCO
CRARRV	Challenger armoured repair and recovery vehicle
EFP	explosively formed projectiles
GPMG	general-purpose machine gun
HMNVS	helmet-mounted night-vision sights
IO	intelligence officer
IPLO	Irish People's Liberation Organisation (republican splinter group)
IRA	Irish Republican Army (also referred to as 'the Provos')
JDAM	Joint Direct Attack Munition
KFOR	Kosovo Force (NATO-led international peacekeeping force)
KOSB	King's Own Scottish Borderers
LAIT	Land Accident Investigation Team (British Army)
MoD	Ministry of Defence
MSG	mobile support group (of the LAIT)

NAAFI	Navy, Army and Air Force Institutes (provides retail and leisure services to the British armed forces)
NAPS	nerve-agent pre-treatment set
NBC	nuclear, biological and chemical
NCO	non-commissioned officer
NITAT	Northern Ireland Training Advisory Team
PRR	personal role radio
QM	quartermaster
RAMC	Royal Army Medical Corps
REME	Royal Electrical and Mechanical Engineers
RMP	Royal Military Police
RPG	rocket-propelled grenade
RQMS	regimental quartermaster sergeant
RSM	regimental sergeant major
RUC	Royal Ulster Constabulary (Northern Ireland police force until 2001)
SAS	Special Air Service
SBS	Special Boat Service
SIB	Special Investigation Branch (of the Royal Military Police)
SLR	self-loading rifle
SO2	staff officer class 2
Stasi	East German Ministry for State Security
SUSAT	Sight Unit Small Arms, Trilux (rifle sight with night vision and four-times magnification)
TESEX	tactical effects simulation exercise
UDF	Ulster Defence Force (loyalist paramilitary group in Northern Ireland)
UDR	Ulster Defence Regiment (British Army regiment in Northern Ireland, formed part of the Royal Irish Regiment in 1992)
VCP	vehicle checkpoint
WO	warrant officer

Prologue
My Day

The crackle of small-arms fire intensified and a bullet pinged off the armour plating on the ambulance behind us. I dropped to a firing position and identified the militiamen through my rifle sights. They were advancing from 800 metres away, some of them wearing red bandanas. They looked like dancers I'd seen once at a Michael Jackson concert.

'No way, Mohammed,' I thought as I took aim. 'This is my day for living, not yours.'

It was 22 March 2003, an unforgettable date. That day, after 20 years' service for Queen and country, I fought the fiercest battle of my life and sent dozens of Iraqis to meet their maker.

• • •

We had crossed the border on 20 March, expecting a massive confrontation. Instead, we passed burning tanks hit by the Americans from the air and roadside positions eerie and deserted save for some abandoned Iraqi helmets and green uniforms.

I was hyped up, raring for battle. As company sergeant major of Charlie Company of the Black Watch regiment, I had responsibility for 200 troops and I knew that this war would be my greatest challenge. I was certain that this conflict was a just one. We hadn't finished the job properly in the first Gulf War. This time we had to remove the tyrant Saddam's finger from the red button that could unleash weapons of mass destruction.

Scud-missile attacks had punctuated our preparations in the Kuwaiti desert. They narrowly missed our camp but forced us, in searing temperatures, to clamber into protective suits and rubber masks, as it was feared that Saddam had the capability to arm Scuds with chemical warheads. For weeks, we had taken a bewildering cocktail of drugs, including anthrax jabs, NAPS (nerve-agent pre-treatment set) tablets and antimalarial pills that gave you nightmares. One day, I had five different injections. We fully believed that we would face chemical and biological attack.

We were cut off from the outside world – two weeks before we invaded, all radio news stations were jammed and the soldiers of the Black Watch Battle Group had to hand in their mobile phones. We were told that using mobile phones might compromise our locations or allow the enemy to tap into conversations, gaining deadly intelligence. This was certainly true but I thought that another factor might be the lack of support for the invasion at home.

Our high morale was tempered by dodgy equipment and a shortage of kit. Many of us went to war wearing heavy black boots and camouflage suits meant for Europe, not for the desert heat, which was magnified in my armoured Warrior Infantry Fighting Vehicle. I was the gunner and relished our one and only opportunity to test-fire the Warrior's weapons – a 30-mm Rarden cannon and a 7.62-mm chain gun – in the desert. Ominously, the gun jammed during the exercise and there were no spares.

I'd already had electric shocks and other problems while training with the Warrior. The chain gun, a machine gun powered electrically from the Warrior's main circuit, had been designed to fit the undercarriage of an American helicopter, where it would be fed rounds by gravity and cooled by the engine's slipstream. Here, the weapon was being used upside down on the scorching turret of the Warrior. The extent of its unsuitability would soon be revealed in the most horrific way.

Our first big objective in Iraq was to capture Az Zubayr, an important oil-refining town and a stronghold of Saddam's Ba'ath Party militia. Then we could move on to the strategically vital city of Basra.

On the morning of 22 March, I was part of an assault group that stormed a large barracks on the edge of Az Zubayr. We were unsure if we would confront Iraqi troops but knew that it was full of munitions. We had four vehicles: two Scimitars (small, armoured reconnaissance vehicles), an ambulance and the Warrior. With me in the Warrior were company commander Major James Ord; our driver, Lance Corporal Lee Kirby; and, in the back of the vehicle, signaller Corporal Mark Calder and company second in command Captain Tim Petransky.

James was to be my strongest ally in this war, the only man I trusted with my life. Despite his posh accent, he was forged of Scottish steel. James had been in the SAS. At his first attempt to join the special-forces regiment, he nearly died on a jungle exercise when he developed pneumonia and his heart stopped. It was testimony to the man's courage that he went straight to the next gruelling selection process and passed. Lee had recently served six months in Colchester military prison for fighting. He was a first-rate driver and soldier, with a dry sense of humour, but he needed keeping in line. Mark was a capable, deep-thinking signaller who had joined us in Kuwait. Tim was also new to the company but our paths had crossed before, in 2000, when he was a cadet at Sandhurst and I was his instructor.

We roared past the black and red flags daubed on the fences leading up to the yellow-painted entrance and kept going until we stumbled across scores of young Iraqis merrily piling up furniture and computers, as well as, alarmingly, anti-tank rockets, sniper rifles and other lethal gear. James stood up in the turret of the Warrior brandishing his rifle. 'British Army! Put down your weapons now!' he yelled in Arabic. We bundled out of our vehicles. With camouflage-painted faces and weapons at the ready, we eventually took control.

The Iraqis comprised two groups. There were the looters, who carried on as if they hadn't noticed us until we slapped a few heads. Maybe they had heard that we'd been ordered not to interfere with their thieving. The rest knew how to handle the weapons they were carrying and were surely militiamen in civilian clothes. We took a robust attitude, firing over their heads at one point.

'Hello, pal, are ye takin' this away for Saddam?' one of the Jocks sarcastically asked a man bearing a sniper rifle. 'I bet ye'll get a couple o' camels for it, ya cheeky bastard.' It was not for nothing that our company, made up of seasoned weapons specialists, was known within the Black Watch as 'the Savages'.

The Jocks laid out a line of captured rocket launchers and long-barrelled rifles and I ordered Lee to drive over them. Then a clearance patrol of nearby buildings discovered two well-stocked armouries. One was crammed with anti-tank weapons, including hundreds of RPGs (rocket-propelled grenades). The other was full of small arms – AK-47s, Dragunov sniper rifles, pistols and masses of small munitions. We cordoned off the area with white mine tape and radioed a call for Royal Engineers to come and blow the lot up, but they were too busy with other skirmishes.

We were amazed that the Iraqi army had abandoned this barracks without a fight. There was enough equipment here to seriously damage our forces. We wondered whether they had expected us to attack in much larger numbers. Later, we learned that their military infrastructure had collapsed. Most of the senior officers had legged it and almost everyone else had jumped out of their uniforms and into civvies. But there were still plenty of men up for a fight.

Our two Scimitars were called away on another mission. Then we came under attack. Momentarily, I was stunned by the sinister crackles and thumps as bullets slapped the ground, buildings and vehicles around us. The looters in the barracks wisely seized the opportunity to scarper. Then my adrenalin surged and I started shooting back. This was the moment we'd been waiting for. These were Saddam's men and their party was over. Big Tam was here to put a stop to their bullying and abuse. Now it was their turn to be exposed to extreme fear before they died. I was consumed with rage.

'Zero Bravo. Contact!' I roared into my radio headset to Lee, who was in the Warrior, as I crouched beside a low wall. 'Myself and Zero Alpha require support. Move to our location now. Out.'

'I'll lay down fire support for you,' shouted James from nearby. Up he stood, all five foot six inches of him, giving the enemy full blast with his SA80 A2 rifle while I clambered onto the Warrior. Then I opened fire with the chain gun, enabling James to join us. 'Sergeant Major, Corporal Kirby – advance, enemy front!' he screamed.

We drove out of the barracks and a little way up the road towards the town, with the ambulance sheltering close behind us. Using my times-eight magnification Raven sight, I got a clearer view of the enemy. Some were grouped outside a building and others were creeping forward on our left, using the sand dunes and rubbish mounds between the barracks and the town as cover. There were probably about fifty men and our training said we'd need another two Warriors to deal with them. But retreat was not an option. If these guys recovered their munitions – especially the anti-tank missiles – they could kill many of our comrades and slow our advance.

'Hello, Zero,' I radioed our HQ, 'this is Zero Bravo. Contact now, Iraqi barracks south of AZ, large numbers of dismounted enemy. We are engaging. Over.' 'Zero. Roger,' came the response. 'Be aware there is no air support available, as it is engaged with the American call signs. Out.'

I was struck by the Iraqis' eclectic dress. Some seemed to be kitted out for a film audition, with their tight trousers, big belt buckles and bandanas. Others were better prepared, wearing combat assault vests designed to carry the battle essentials of bombs, bullets and water. But all were well armed, with AK-47s, RPG launchers and the rest.

A man in police uniform caught my attention. He was plainly directing the 'extras' from the edge of the town. I took my time tracking him with the Rarden cannon before firing a high-explosive shell. He disappeared on impact.

A group dashed into a nearby house and started shooting at us.

'Check out these guys. They've just gone into that house with the big yellow door.'

'Engage!' James replied.

I sang an adapted snatch of the Shakin' Stevens hit 'Green Door'. 'There's an old piano and they play it hot behind the yellow door.' My shell hit the door and destroyed the house.

Another shot went straight through a telegraph pole, leaving a perfect hole. 'Look at the circle in that pole. Is that sharp shooting or what?' James and I paused to discuss this. Later on, our guys who were stuck in the back said it had been scary listening to our calm conversation, not knowing whether we would get through the day.

While the cannon was used against buildings and vehicles, the chain gun dealt more effectively with men on the move, spewing out 600 rounds a minute. Despite the manic tension, it was a fairly clinical process. James might shout, 'Enemy left, traverse left,' and I would move the turret to the left with a thumb-operated switch. 'Steady on' meant that we had the enemy in our sights. I'd release the safety mechanism and announce, 'Chain gun on firing now.' Then I'd press down on the foot-firing switch and watch the devastating results as men went spinning into the air. James would say, 'Target destroyed. Target stop,' I'd put the safety catch back on and we'd search for the next target.

Then the chain gun jammed, as had happened so often on the firing ranges. We briefly withdrew a little, firing the cannon while I quickly fixed it. We were under relentless assault from groups trying to bypass us and get into the barracks or simply to wipe us out. We had to protect the ambulance, which had taken several bullet hits. RPGs kept whooshing past us and exploding nearby. Twice, the enemy scored direct hits, their warheads bouncing off the nose-cone of the Warrior, making it shake sickeningly. If they hit us from closer range, we would fry.

For about an hour, we jockeyed back and forth, with Lee skilfully dodging the rockets as I sought to kill those who dispatched them.

Then the chain gun jammed again. I kept kicking the foot-firing switch but got no response. 'Stoppage!' I screamed. James boldly stood up in the turret and sprayed the enemy with rifle fire while I desperately stripped down the chain gun. My hands dripped blood, as I grappled with scorching, sharp-edged metal, but I became oblivious to the pain, entranced in my work. If I dropped one tiny component, we would all die.

'Stoppage!'

'Fuck!' I threw up my rifle to James and it started to clatter comfortingly.

Then again: 'Stoppage!'

A glance through the sights showed that at least one RPG party was getting dangerously close. Maybe this was the final curtain. At least I had got the chain gun reassembled. 'Please God,' I mouthed as I pressed down with my right foot. 'Bollocks!' I pressed down again. The chain gun groaned and started to turn. 'Thank fuck for that.' I grinned broadly at James and neutralised the RPG team.

But the enemy kept advancing. They seemed unstoppable. No matter how many I killed, more kept coming. Our chain gun might fail again at any time. I'd had enough. 'We need to fix bayonets, dismount and deal with these arseholes,' I bawled. 'Move forward now,' I ordered Lee.

James didn't rate this as my brightest idea. 'You're pissed,' he said.

Lee shouted something indecipherable and we lurched not forwards but sharply backwards, bashing into the front of the ambulance.

'What is Kirby doing?'

Then an RPG flew past my eyes. Lee had saved our lives. I swivelled the turret to the right and chain-gunned the ambushers.

'Very brave but very dead,' I said. I respected this enemy. They were hardcore fighters, probably part of the elite Republican Guard. They saw what our weapons could do to them but, like us, they were loyal to a code and defied the natural instinct to run for cover. We had locked horns over a conflicting but identical goal. It was man against man, blood against blood.

Hours passed but my sense of time melted in the furnace of the battle. I never thought to eat and, although I had water and was sweating profusely, I dismissed my growing thirst as a distraction. It was stifling inside the Warrior, with the heat and dust and the whiff of cordite. Sandy sweat obscured my vision and the salt from my perspiration turned my combats white. We were enveloped in a deafening cacophony of engine, guns, enemy bullets and RPGs, and our yells to each other and our base.

At last, word came that a Warrior from Delta Company was joining us, carrying plastic explosives to blow up the Iraqi armouries. We made some decisions. James would go back into the barracks with three men to destroy the munitions. The other Warrior couldn't stay and it would take the ambulance with it when it left. I would withdraw to near the entrance and keep blasting at all comers.

I wished James good luck and scanned the troubling horizon. Suddenly, I chuckled aloud. I'd taken James's headset when he dismounted, to allow me to contact HQ, and I'd fitted a PRR (personal role radio) under my Warrior headset so that I could speak to James on the ground. Here I was with three headsets squeezed under my helmet. I must have looked like something out of Billy Smart's Circus. A familiar voice dispersed these clownish thoughts. 'Hello, Zero Bravo, this is Zero. Can you give me an estimate of enemy numbers?'

'I'm not exactly sure,' I replied, 'but you'll need to bring a couple of double-deckers to pick them up.'

I'd spotted new forces gathering near the buildings. They must have thought we were in retreat. Some were climbing into technicals – pick-up trucks adapted for battle with fixed machine guns. The first one set off down the road to the barracks. 'Here we go,' I grunted. I'd trained for two years hitting fast-moving targets. Time slowed as I calmly fired the cannon and watched flames leap triumphantly from the truck. Two more technicals took to the road and I obliterated them spectacularly. It felt surreal, like starring in a slow-motion scene from an action movie. I glanced up at a photo of my daughter Hannah that I had pinned to the turret. Yes, it had to be my day to live.

I fought on, targeting and shooting at Iraqi soldiers, who ran and ducked behind the sand dunes. Three more times, the chain gun died on me but each time, with a pounding heart, I was able to quickly revive the weapon.

Despite my vigilance, a sizeable militia group managed to get past me on my right flank. Others kept pressing forwards.

'Hello, Zero Alpha, this is Zero Bravo. Over,' I radioed James. 'The enemy has breached and is in the barracks. Are you finished?'

'Another five minutes.'

Jesus. I couldn't hold them off for ever. Minutes now seemed like hours. No word from James. Then the radio spluttered. 'Task complete. We are engaging enemy dismounts. RV [rendezvous] at the armouries ASAP.' We reversed over the barracks fence, swung around and sped to where James and his men were trading bullets with the enemy. 'We've got three minutes to get out of here,' James bellowed. The Warrior slowed but kept moving as they ran and clambered aboard.

'Right, who won the loudest-shouting competition?' beamed James, with his helmet half off. We accelerated towards the railway track, away from the town. I swivelled the turret to watch the Iraqis flood forward, guns held aloft. Then the ground shook. Two low booms resounded and fireballs leapt from the barracks a hundred metres into the air, followed by a giant shroud of smoke.

We were jubilant.

'Yes! Fuck you, Saddam!'

We'd been fighting for seven hours and had a party on the way back. Sweets and water were passed up, along with more ammunition in case we got ambushed.

Back at the Black Watch Battle Group base – tents and armoured vehicles in the sand, surrounded by a ring of tanks – I prepared the Warrior for its next shift, removing thousands of empty bullet cases and inspecting the RPG scorch marks and bullet-chipped paint. Exhausted, I sat and pondered in the warm darkness. Noisy, vivid scenes of fire and death flitted through my mind.

Until that day, I had not taken a single life, although I had been involved in several conflicts. I knew somehow that I was changed for ever. Some people say that soldiers are trained to do anything, without scruples. But the truth is simply that we can find ourselves in situations where we have to kill or die, and everyday rules don't apply. As I was to find out, men can become dangerously conditioned to this.

I wondered about the families of the dead – the mothers, wives, young children. 'God forgive me and look after them,' I prayed. But I believed in our cause and knew that we had saved the lives of many of our men. It was a year since my driver, Private Rab Donkin – a superb young soldier – had been killed in Macedonia after I sent him on a mission. I had sworn to do my utmost to prevent anything similar happening again.

Never before had I seen such bravery as my commander's, standing up in the turret and then fearlessly returning to the barracks on foot. I decided I would recommend him for a medal. As it turned out, however, I would be unable to do this: the military establishment that I had loyally served was about to skewer me.

ONE

Forget All Our Troubles

Stobhill Hospital's leaky roof was a godsend. It gave Philip a cold and so the nurses told Anne that she could keep her baby for a whole week before she had to give him away, not just for the two days she had been told she would have. The 19 year old held her son close, relishing every moment. The radio played a hit that would make her cry in the years to come: 'Downtown' by Petula Clark, with its bittersweet lyrics, promising 'we can forget all our troubles'. It was their song, hers and Philip's.

When the day came to hand him over, Anne was distraught. Shivering and sobbing, she was led to a room, carrying Philip, wrapped in a shawl, for the last time. From next door, she could hear the voices of the people who were taking him. Then the man from St Margaret's Adoption Society came in and she screwed her eyes shut as he lifted her son from her arms.

She knew that she must get away from Glasgow. What if she bumped into the couple who had taken Philip, pushing him in a pram? For her, the city held nothing but bad memories. Abandoned as a child to the care of the Nazarene nuns, she had now been pressed into giving up her little boy. Anne fled to London, where she fell in love with a fellow Glaswegian, Stewart McFarlane. She knew he was the man for her when he said, 'Let's go together and get your baby back.' But it was hopeless. The adoption society could not help.

Philip had been made a ward of court and Anne had no legal right of access. She was told she had best forget about him.

• • •

Philip McEwan, born 19 February 1967, became Thomas Henderson. Most people called me Tam. My new parents, Jessie and Pat, took me the ten miles to their little house on Benson Street in Whifflet, Coatbridge. We lived downstairs and a retired couple lived upstairs. Old Mr McManus was ex-army and seemed strict. From an early age, I kept well clear of him.

A decade before I came along, my mum Jessie had lost a baby and they'd told her she might die if she tried for another. She was determined to do her best for me but Pat was gone by the time I was three and a half. I have no early memories of him, though I later learned that he was a big gambler. Shortly after he left, Pat borrowed money in Mum's name and the bailiffs called, threatening to take our furniture. She sold it all to pay the debt and bought two plane tickets to Canada with the rest. Before we got on the plane, Mum bought me a new pair of sandals. Their shiny plastic smell has stayed with me and always reminds me of my first flight. In Toronto, we met Mum's two sisters and lots of cousins. I began speaking with a Canadian accent. But after just seven months, Pat charmed Jessie back home to Glasgow and our new life was over. Mum was a romantic and a good Catholic, believing that a husband and wife should stay married until the grave.

Her faith was rewarded when she quickly became pregnant and safely gave birth to my brother Bob. But then Pat ran off again. I remember one day I was playing in Mum's room when she came in very upset. I hid under her bed as she sat crying, stifling my own tears of sympathy and confusion. We moved in with one of her brothers, Robert. My uncle was more like a father to me, a fine role model who always worked hard and treated people with respect. I loved to sit beside him watching John Wayne films on the TV. After the film was over, I'd run out into the street to play with my cowboy hat and toy pistol. Robert worked for Dunlop's, the tyre manufacturers, with his three brothers. When the factory was relocated to Birmingham in 1972, we followed it.

It was a seismic change, from a village of familiar faces to a sprawling council estate in Hamstead, Great Barr, full of Irish, Indians, Pakistanis, West Indians, Geordies and Scots, all speaking with different accents. I didn't hear many Brummies. We packed into a three-bedroom council house: my Uncle Robert, Mum, Bob and me, Uncle Jimmy, Auntie Moira and their children, Robert and Alison. Uncle Andy would also come to stay.

It took Mum months to get us into a Catholic school, so we started at the local state school, where I enjoyed mixing with kids from different cultures. Then we went to the local Catholic primary school, staffed by some fearsome nuns. One sister would hit kids on the backs of their knees with her ruler and I remember being dragged by my hair to the front of the class for a beating. Monday-morning assemblies could be scary. Sometimes they made an example of kids who had missed Mass the day before. One day, it was my turn.

'What did Father talk about in his sermon yesterday?'

'I don't know, Sister.'

Off I went for a whacking from the headmistress, whose calves were as big as my head. It wasn't fair. Mum worked on Sundays and there was no way I was walking the ten-mile round-trip to the church beside the school. It was a hike I already made most schooldays, spending my two-pence bus fare on sweets. I wasn't going to do it on God's day of rest! But it was the norm for teachers to hit children and there was no point telling Mum about it. Anyway, there were lots of good times to cancel out the bad. I toured the county with the junior cricket team and played Joseph in the nativity play. Caroline Jordan was a lovely Mary.

Mum juggled two jobs, as a barmaid and a cleaner, and she later got a van and delivered meat for a butcher. In 1976, when I was nine, the three of us moved into a first-floor maisonette, with ten flats to a landing and everywhere the din of boisterous kids, rowing neighbours and barking, defecating dogs. The flat was on the Durham Estate, originally built for miners from the North-east. It was a hard place, ruled by rival gangs. I was the only kid going to the 'posh' Catholic school and needed eight stitches in my chin one day after I was attacked on my way home. But at least we had a place of our own – until the man whom I'll call Terry appeared.

My first memory of him is the smell of stale alcohol and the sight of his bare chest and tattooed arms in Mum's bed. 'Mum!' I shouted, and she came out of the bathroom and shut the bedroom door. He was in his early 30s, a few years younger than Mum. She didn't know many people down south and he took her out to meet his family and friends. But I sensed that he was trouble. He put on a charade for Mum, pretending to like me and Bob, but went cold as soon as she left the room.

My resentment towards the intruder turned to hatred on Christmas Day 1976, when he took off his shoe to thump me on my elbow and knee while Mum was in the kitchen. 'Keep your fucking mouth shut or I'll smack your head in,' he hissed.

Two days later, Mum yelled from the kitchen, 'Thomas!' I dashed in to find him pushing her over the sink with his hands around her throat. He let go but an open war had begun.

They married on 10 May 1977 and my hostility boiled over at the reception at the local miners' club, where I tugged at a tablecloth, sending sausage rolls and cakes flying. Mum took me outside for a good talking to. I didn't care. I knew we were all in for a bad time. After the wedding, Terry started taking control. He banned me from going out without his permission and ruled that we couldn't get up until he said so. It was awful, having to stay in bed on a Sunday morning while he recovered from a hangover. Bob and I felt like prisoners.

Terry was a local tough guy. If he had a job, I don't know what it was. Thickset, he was proud of his beer belly, which he would push out over his trousers, pretending to be pregnant. That was his idea of a laugh. He had learned how to treat women by seeing his father routinely batter his mother. When Mum told him not to pick on me, he turned on her savagely. Bob and I were sent out of the living room and had to listen to Mum screaming as he lashed out with fist, boot and fire poker. He'd roll in drunk and, after hurting Mum, drag Bob and me from under our duvets for a thumping. Some nights, the police came and Mum begged them to take him away but they refused to get involved. 'Sort out your own problems,' they said.

It pissed me off that almost no one tried to help us, though people knew what was happening. One day, Uncle Robert came to talk to him and I howled as my favourite uncle, just five foot four and fifteen years older than Terry, kicked back as he took a beating.

'You call me Dad,' Terry ordered me daily. But I knew my dad was a man called Pat Henderson who lived in Scotland. Bob and I would go with Mum to see him twice a year. Those were happy days. Pat would take us to the seaside or we would visit Granny Henderson, who plied us with hugs and sweets. Pat wasn't a good father but at least he wasn't violent. Sometimes, when Terry was raging, I'd lie in bed sobbing, 'Dad, Dad, please come and get us.' I secretly wrote him letters – that was another banned activity. They helped me dream of another life, away from the monster.

One morning, when I was 12, all my hopes were shattered. After another row with my mum, Terry stormed off to lie down on my bed. Then we heard him roar, 'What the fuck's this?' I sat shaking in the living room as he hurtled down with the pencilled sheets of the letter I'd hidden under my pillow.

'Leave him alone,' said Mum.

'Do you want me to tell him the truth?'

'No, Terry, don't tell him, please don't tell him!'

'Tell me what?' I demanded.

'He's not your fucking dad!'

That's how I found out. My mum wasn't really my mum and my dad was just some guy she'd been married to. It felt like I'd been malleted. After Terry stomped out to the pub, Mum cuddled me and talked to me, trying to soften the blow, but I couldn't take it in. I didn't know who I was any more. All I knew was that I didn't belong here.

When I got into trouble soon after, Terry exerted his fatherly influence by punching me in the jaw and then slapping me so hard as I ate that the knife tore into my cheek. Once I was big enough, I decided, I would kill him. He started picking more on Bob, who was four years younger and I tried my best to defend my brother against our sadistic stepfather. Terry's reign of terror was waning, however. In spilling the beans about my adoption, he had lost the upper hand. Mum was determined to get rid of him.

One Saturday, Mum left us at Uncle Robert's. I was terrified for her and scarcely slept. In the morning, I dashed back to our flat. When Mum opened the door, I took one look at her and dropped to my knees in horror, hugging her legs.

'You bastard!' I screamed up the stairs.

'It's all right, he's gone,' she said. Mum looked like something from a horror film, with a line of black stitches down one side of her partly shaven head, two black eyes and a broken nose. 'I knew he would do this to me,' she explained, 'but it was the only way I could get him out of the house.'

My plucky mum had sat waiting for him to stumble home in a drunken stupor. When he attacked her as usual, she resisted with all her slender strength. So he picked up a glass ashtray and tried to stave her head in. This time when the police came, they took him away and called an ambulance for Mum. She'd had to risk being murdered for them to do anything. I combed Mum's hair, trying to make her look less frightening before Bob came home. I'll never forget how brave she was that day – a lioness defending her cubs. She's always been an inspiration to us both. Mum took out an injunction against Terry and, while it wasn't the last we saw of him, it was the end of a catastrophic period.

By now, I was running with a multiracial gang based at the south end of the estate. I had my first snog with the sister of our leader. He went on to join the police. We fought fiercely with sticks against other gangs, smoked, sniffed glue and stole from shop lock-ups. Younger ones like me acted as lookouts and helped to hide the loot. One day, we got caught with stolen goods and, aged 12, I was driven in a police Allegro to the station, where I was strip-searched and charged with theft.

Six of us, including my cousin Robert, found ourselves sitting with our mums on a wooden bench at the juvenile court. Fortunately, I had a part-time job; otherwise, I might have been sent to a detention centre. Instead, I spent many Saturdays at the Smethwick Attendance Centre, where retired soldiers and policemen taught us woodwork. There were some huge black gang leaders from Handsworth in the senior classes trying to run the show but I'd had enough of being bullied and held my own in several fights.

One of the probation officers wanted to help me mend my fractured sense of identity. He got social services to investigate my adoption and I got slivers of information. A letter from the St Margaret's Adoption Society told me that my natural mother was called Anne. She came from Glasgow and had been an unmarried teenage waitress when she'd had me. It said she ran away after I was adopted and they didn't know where she was. This was strangely comforting. It made me think that maybe she hadn't been happy to give me up. My father, apparently, was tall and blond with blue eyes. That's all I've ever heard about him.

I still loved my mum Jessie but was full of resentment. 'When were you going to tell me?' I'd ask her. Of course, she'd been scared of hurting me but it stung me to find out that almost everyone in the family – all my uncles and cousins – had known except me. I understand now that she felt very guilty about how my early life turned out. Through no fault of hers, I hadn't enjoyed the stability that adoption is meant to offer. Sometimes I'd hurt my mum, saying, 'I know you love me, even though I am adopted.'

I was leading a double life now, running with wolves on my estate and gambolling with lambs at school. I craved both danger and culture, and got them. At school, I joined the orchestra and played the double bass. Stuart Bathurst was a good Catholic secondary. No one else from my estate went there and I stood out like a sore thumb – the only kid on free school meals. But some of the teachers really cared. Mr Finch and Mr Kelly were very encouraging and I felt I'd let them down by getting into trouble with the law.

And there was Julie Goldby. She was the darling of our year – the girl with the sparkling smile and lovely legs, hugged by her school skirt. Her friend Helen Magee told me that Julie fancied me and so I nervously asked her out to the cinema. We started going out together at 14. My life suddenly became much happier. We loved each other, in our young way. Julie often took me back to her large house – her dad was a builder – and I became friends with the whole family.

Work also gave me stability. I progressed from a paper round to a milk round and on to the city-centre rag markets, where I could make £3 a night after school and a fabulous £60 at weekends. I was able to take Julie to the pub for her first drink and buy her a £30 jacket. It could be wild at the market, with Gypsies, West Indians and Pakistanis fighting over pitches, but, thankfully, it dragged me away from the gangs, taught me about teamwork and built my self-esteem.

Many of the kids at school were determined to do A levels but I had a very different plan. All my uncles had done national service in the army and they often reminisced about the camaraderie and the laughs. It was great discipline and a great life, they said. The only photo Mum had of her dad was of a cavalryman in khaki uniform, mounted on his horse with an ammunition bandolier across his chest. As my brother Bob got older, he grew to look the spit of him.

Good at sport, adventurous and determined, I knew I could be a soldier. More importantly, it was a way out of my life in Birmingham. I didn't belong on our shitty council estate. I wanted to embrace my roots – my Scottish heritage. And what better way than by joining the famous kilt-wearing, bagpiping 'screaming Jock' regiment. I devoured books about it in the school library. It had distinguished itself in a multitude of battles and its soldiers were a breed apart. Uncle Robert said the Germans had called them 'devils in skirts'. They were the finest fighting force on earth. I didn't just want to sign up to the army: I wanted to join the Black Watch.

My older cousin John Paul had joined the navy and in 1982 he sailed with the task force sent to expel the Argentinians from the Falklands. At 15, I sat glued to the news footage showing the romantic send-off. I was transfixed by the Battle of Goose Green and other British triumphs. Then a recruitment officer, a captain from the Guards, came to our school with a smart team of boys. He gave a video presentation, showing the glamour of our South Atlantic victory and the promise of lots of foreign travel and skiing. I waited behind in the hall to collect leaflets and we talked about my cousin, the Falklands War, my job and my role in the school football team. 'You're just the sort of chap we're looking for,' he said.

At the army careers office in town, I spilled the beans on my biggest worry – my criminal record. But it turned out that my conviction was spent and wouldn't affect my recruitment. Over the next nine months, I sat several tests in numeracy, literacy and reasoning. I was the only kid in my class doing this; most were from stable homes and didn't see the army as a good career. But I wanted a new life.

In May 1983, I was summoned to a three-day selection event for the Infantry Junior Leaders Battalion. I'd gone for the infantry because I wanted to be in the thick of it. If I succeeded, I'd probably become an NCO and have a good chance to commission. I was 16 and destiny was calling me. Excited, I took the train to London and another to Aldershot. The station thronged with Welsh Guards proudly wearing T-shirts bearing the words 'Falklands War'. I couldn't wait to get on the minibus to the barracks at North Camp.

That night, I heard one lad crying for his mum. What's he doing here? I thought. From my job on the market, I was used to being independent and familiar with hard physical work, putting up heavy frames for the canopies, getting soaked to the skin, getting on with it. Although I was skinny, I knew I was very fit. This was my big opportunity and I concentrated on making a bloody good impression and showing the army that I was exactly what they wanted. The selection process involved paper tests, physical tests, interviews and medicals. I did my best at everything and was chuffed to come first in the cross-country race. In the interviews, they asked me about everything: my family, school and my trouble with the police. I told them that my sights were firmly set on the Black Watch.

We were a mixed bunch of lads and the competition was fierce. Not all of us would make it. I was one of the few who weren't in the army cadets and had never marched up and down a square before but I lapped it all up. It was everything I wanted. Even the cookhouse food tasted delicious! I wasn't an extrovert but discovered that I could fit in effortlessly. I was used to mixing with people from different backgrounds. If people wanted to talk to me about fighting – or music, religion, Scotland, whatever – I could hold my own.

At last we were summoned, one by one, to learn our fate. 'We are very pleased with your performance, Henderson,' said the sergeant major, a stereotypical sort with a clipped voice and moustache. (It rankled, being called by my surname. At school, I was 'Thomas' to the teachers. It was something about the army that would piss me off every day for years to come.) 'We have a guaranteed vacancy for you,' he went on, 'but you can't join a Scottish regiment.'

'Why not, sir?' I asked.

He was taken aback and claimed that the rules said I had to join the regiment nearest to where I lived – the Staffordshire Regiment.

'But I've never heard of them. I don't want to join them!'

'Well, Henderson, if you want to join the army you have to join the Staffs.'

Back in Birmingham, I ran into opposition at home. Life was better for Mum by then. We'd moved away from the flats and into a council house. She had kept quiet when I'd said I wanted to join the army. Perhaps she'd secretly hoped I wouldn't get through and would be content to stay at home for a while in our nice council house, peaceful at last. She tried to put her foot down when I produced the paperwork for her to sign. 'You're too young, son.' I know now that she was thinking about the dark side of the Falklands War, the dead and maimed. Of course she didn't want to lose me. But I was so set on the army that I didn't care about hurting her. I threatened to join under my own steam when I was 18 and never come home again. She signed.

Julie wasn't happy either. I'd thought she would understand. She hadn't said anything before and her older brother was a soldier. But because of my youth, my application had taken more than a year. Perhaps she'd thought it might never happen. I also think she wanted to take our kissing further, though, as a good Catholic boy, I wasn't sure I was ready for that. We both cried when we parted after one too many rows about the army.

My boss on the markets tried to tempt me to stay with the offer of promotion and more money. Dave Everett was a great boss (he went on to become a millionaire, selling his market business and setting up an equestrian centre) but I was set upon following my own path.

Aged 16, I proudly enlisted at the West Bromwich army careers office, swearing an oath of allegiance to the Queen and collecting my rail warrant to Folkestone, along with a five-pound note as the 'Queen's shilling'. The enlisting major, who had commissioned through the ranks, spoke of the joys of army life. I was through the door now and determined somehow to find my way into the Black Watch.

TWO

Virgin Soldier

'**D**on't do it! There's no escape!' Squaddies hung out of windows screaming at us as we marched up the long road. This was our welcome to the Sir John Moore Barracks at Shorncliffe, near Folkestone, where the Infantry Junior Leaders Battalion was based. It trained young men for every infantry regiment in the British Army. The sheer size of the place was intimidating. To our left was a three-deep line of grey, six-storey dormitory blocks and to our right a green sea of rugby and football pitches.

Shortly after we reached our fourth-floor dormitory, the fire alarm blared and everyone poured onto the giant asphalt parade square for a roll call. As new boys, we were eyeballed by uniformed soldiers who, though only slightly older, seemed massive. I felt like an ant on parade. The unspoken message from on high was: 'Look around you. This is your new family. Do you really want to be here?' In those days, if you didn't or if you weren't up to it, they wanted rid of you. Of the 52 who joined the Peninsula Company's 17 Platoon with me, only 19 passed out at the end of the year.

I kept quiet at first, just saying hello to my immediate neighbours: Baptiste, a black guy in the bunk beside me, 'Taff' and 'Ginge'. Everyone in the army has a nickname. I got mine straight away from our NCO, Corporal Steve Narbett, a little Brummie with a pencil moustache.

'What's your name?' he asked me.

'Henderson, sir.'

'What fucking accent is that?'

'Scottish, sir.'

'Where are you from?'

'Birmingham, sir.'

'Are you taking the piss? Why aren't you up the road with the other Jocks?'

'I was told I can't join the Black Watch because I live in England, sir.'

'Well, I hate smelly socks. You're better off here. And make sure you get your hair cut, you Jock hippy.'

I'd grown up speaking with two accents, Glasgow Scottish at home and Brummie everywhere else, but I abandoned my adopted dialect the moment I left the city. As the Staffordshire Regiment's only Jock at Shorncliffe, I was an individual of interest. This did me no harm, although some NCOs greeted me with 'Och aye the noo' and made me do press-ups for being Scottish. I later learned that our platoon sergeant, Chris Claus, was the son of a Black Watch soldier who had settled in Staffordshire. Chris was a very professional and fair-minded man. His bearing was rigidly upright. Wherever he walked, he marched and whenever he talked, it was army talk. He had a positive influence on us all and, of course, I put this down to his breeding. Years later, I would teach his son at Sandhurst.

'How would you like it, sir?' asked the army barber, tongue firmly in cheek, before he attacked my shoulder-length hair, cropping it to my skull. I had always worn it long and I thought the new haircut made my head look like a peanut.

On day two, we were issued with uniforms and PE kit for our first gym session. I felt like a scarecrow in my flat-soled flapping plimsolls, Stanley Matthews shorts with protruding string and long red vest, the clothes hanging off my skinny frame. It became a feature of army life – everything was always too big or too small for me.

Day four was 'milling' (fighting) time, when we were paired off for bouts of 'technical boxing' in the ring. You were meant to be matched for weight and height but my opponent seemed a foot taller than me.

'I'm the under-18s karate champion for Wales,' he boasted as we queued up to batter each other.

'Book me an ambulance!' I shouted to the other lads, stepping into the ring and pretending to climb out the other side.

'Box!' ordered the referee as we stood toe to toe. Lofty swiftly clubbed me on the nose. Knowing nothing of the noble art, I lost my temper and started windmilling him until he fell over. When he got up, I pummelled his face until the referee pulled me away.

Later, I was ordered to see Lieutenant Phipps, a bear of a man. 'Henderson, you're a bit of an animal,' he said. 'And you're in the boxing team.'

'I don't want to join the boxing team, sir.' It meant two extra hours' training in an already hectic schedule.

'Shut up, Henderson, and do a hundred press-ups.'

'Yes, sir.'

'And you're in the team, Henderson.'

'Yes, sir,' I replied from the floor near his feet.

It was a harsh induction delivering a blunt message: this is the army – expect to see blood, get hurt and deliver pain. However, I had won a good place in the battalion's newly forged pecking order. All in all, it was an excellent first week.

Most of the Junior Leaders came from army families and had been cadets. Wearing uniform, marching and saluting came naturally to them. Some had been to army public schools like the Duke of York's Royal Military School. But I had other advantages. I'd learned discipline working in the rag market and I swiftly adapted to the strain of living in a room with nine other guys all sharing the same toilet and washing and shaving as ordered, even if we didn't need to.

Marching became like breathing as our synchronised boots daily bashed tarmac, halted, turned around and stood at ease. On parade, individuals were called out and ordered to recite the full names and ranks of our superior officers. 'Bed blocks' became more important than breakfast. Every morning, our beds, lockers and boots were inspected by NCOs expecting to see all our sleeves crisply facing the same way, our boots gleaming and our blankets and sheets parcelled into pristine squares – bed blocks – that you could bounce a ball off.

If they weren't, they threw them out the window and they might trample on your boots for good measure when you ran outside to recover your stuff. Then you had to report to the guardroom for inspection at 10 p.m. and stay up getting your kit ready for the next day. Some guys just slept on the floor to avoid the hassle each morning. My bedding went flying a few times but I had an eye for detail and, with a mum who juggled three jobs, I knew how to wash, clean and iron. Baptiste was hopeless with the bed blocks, so I would make his while he bulled my boots. Such cooperation was common, reflecting our burgeoning team spirit.

I'm sure that some of the NCOs had dirt on their gloves so they could soil someone's gear and put him on report. In my experience, they didn't need to use violence when they could issue terrifying threats and make 16-year-old boys jump around like frogs and do press-ups until their already blistered hands bled. However, we were lucky to be in the charge of some decent men like Sergeant Claus and Corporal Narbett, whose fierce words lacked real menace. Any bullying at Sir John Moore was comparatively muted.

After the Falklands War, the top brass concluded that they needed fitter troops and, by today's standards, our training was intensive from the outset. We did five-mile runs with heavy kit, tackled assault courses and handled a range of weapons, including the 7.62-mm SLR (the 'elephant gun'), the 84-mm anti-tank gun, a beast that took two people to fire, and the general-purpose machine gun (GPMG), which could demolish a building.

On our first 'frolic' (night exercise), near the Folkestone cliffs, we built basic shelters called 'bashas' and spent the night in them. While I dutifully hung my uniform on branches and stood my boots and socks neatly beside my shelter, the whizz-kid former cadets knew to keep everything in their sleeping bags. The next day was a clammy lesson in the importance of always keeping my kit dry.

At the start of the exercise, the NCOs made us sit on the grass waiting for our ration packs. We were to choose from a tempting array of boxes introduced to us seductively by Corporal Narbett. 'What have we here?' he said, opening boxes and pulling out the contents. 'Twenty Benson & Hedges and a bottle of plonk – with a glass. Don't ever say we don't fucking look after you! And look here! A box of After Eight mints.' Of course, these goodies were being pulled out of boxes with false bottoms, positioned above holes in the grass, and we were dismayed to discover that what our boxes really held was stuff like corned beef, dry biscuits and porridge. The corporals had a hoot at our expense and the message was clear: this was no holiday camp.

I passed all the physical and mental tests, sometimes coming first. Our results were always pinned to a board, exposing failure and success. As one of the fittest recruits and a quick learner, I fully expected to pass the first six-week stage of our selection. Then I almost blew it. We were on a gruelling end-of-term exercise that involved marching for miles with heavy gear, coming under simulated attack, having to counter-attack and setting up camp at midnight in the pouring rain. We tried to grab some kip in our wet sleeping bags in between doing stags (shifts on sentry duty). At about four, we were woken by thunderflashes, stun grenades, smoke bombs and whistles. We had been warned that we would be 'bugged out' at some point but we were still shocked. Following instructions, I grabbed my rifle and kitbag and hastened to the agreed assembly point. As an acting section commander, I brought my eight-man team with me.

Lieutenant Phipps was a humourless guy who always looked like he'd just lost his mother. He made us kneel on the sloping, muddy ground and was directly in front of me as he gave the order: 'Right, you arseholes, check that your safety catches are on!' For some reason, I pulled the trigger instead. Fortunately, we had no live rounds but the residue peppered Phipps' backside, making him jump in the air before he swung around and yanked me up by the throat. 'You Jock twat!' He punched me in the chest and I went flying backwards. Two more guns were fired by mistake and the staff went crazy, running us out of the camp and making us walk until daylight while they kept shouting at us.

Later that morning, I was marched in front of the company commander, Major Young. 'Henderson, you cunt,' he spat. 'You disgust me. You are meant to shoot the enemy, not your own people.' He found me guilty of a negligent discharge and imposed a £25 fine. I was marched out, devastated by this blow to my career and wallet.

Sergeant Claus took me into his office. 'Look, Henderson,' he said, 'you need to put this behind you. The major wants to see you again.'

Back we went and I stood to attention, expecting another bollocking. 'Well done, Henderson,' said the major, as if our previous encounter had never happened. 'You've had an excellent six weeks. You're one of the few we see here with real leadership potential and I'm making you junior lance corporal.'

Had he been smoking his socks? I expected a circus trumpeter to jump out of the cupboard, play a few toots and shout 'Only joking!' before they all set about me. Instead, the major attached a stripe to my uniform, to the applause of the sergeant, the corporal and the lieutenant I had shot in the arse. It was my first promotion. With huge pride, I replaced my combat hat (we called it the 'crap hat') with a beret showing that I had passed the first stage. Failures were back-squadded: they had to start all over again or drop out. I was going resolutely forwards, one of just three recruits in our platoon elevated to junior lance corporal.

At 16, I was thrilled to be allowed to drink the beer in the NAAFI club, where I mixed with junior NCOs from all the other regiments. We were the crème de la crème and I soaked up advice from those who were a bit older and knew the ropes. The army was my family now. I utterly belonged and wanted to follow a golden career path, become a distinguished soldier, fight battles and earn good money.

After ten weeks, I had my first leave and headed back to Birmingham for a fortnight, feeling like Rambo and keen to let down my imaginary hair. My monthly salary was £240 and, since we were only given £7 a week on camp, I had an incredible £600 in my new Abbey National account. Mum was doing well. I took her out for a couple of meals and was chuffed to hear of her plan to set up a taxi firm. She was calling it T&R Cars, after me and Bob.

Keen to impress my old pals, I hit the town. But it turned out that we were already in different worlds. The lads from the estate couldn't relate to my new experiences and had few of their own to talk about. My mates from the market were happily ducking and diving but I had joined a different team. Even my accent was different to theirs now. I concentrated on getting pissed and trying to chat up girls. The old bonds were melting. Sometimes I felt angry, thinking that while I was training to defend liberty and fight for my country, others were wasting their lives.

I couldn't wait to get back to camp. My best mates now were my fellow junior NCOs, 'Shady' Kent and Dave Reading. Dave was a big lad who loved his grub but very fit. There was a lot of friendly competition between us. It was a thrill when Dave's dad, who was in the SAS, visited him, back from Afghanistan and full of tales of training the mujahideen to fight the Russians.

As junior non-commissioned officers, we could now lead men on parade. When the winter passed, I enjoyed leading my section on ten-mile marches along Folkestone's shoreline, where we would halt at the topless beach, marching on the spot and admiring the scenery. There were tits everywhere – I had never seen anything like it! We felt like SAS heroes but no doubt the women just saw a bunch of 16- and 17-year-old lads on heat.

The second and third terms at Shorncliffe were a blur of relentless activity and excitement. Going skiing in Norway was a highlight, my first trip abroad since Mum had taken me to Canada. It proved to me that the army kept the promises it made when it was recruiting. I fractured a wrist and came back in plaster but clutching a silver medal. Observing a simulated battle at a huge army range at Warminster was spectacular, another great experience. We were given a stirring taste of warfare, with ground troops and mock artillery, tank and aircraft fire – but without the gore. Digging trenches in the French snow – highly arduous work – was less appealing, as was NBC (nuclear, biological and chemical) warfare training.

This involved running around in charcoal-lined suits and respirators, and being briefly exposed to the acrid sting of CS gas in a packed chamber above the Folkestone cliffs. The instructors made us remove our respirators and wouldn't let us out until we'd recited our names and numbers.

'24683084 Junior Lance Corporal Henderson,' I shouted, trying not to inhale.

'I can't hear you!' the instructor kept yelling, until I was choking.

My first glimpse of a real live Black Watch soldier came shortly after I arrived at Shorncliffe. Bristling with aggression, Sergeant Willie Boyle marched onto the parade square in his immaculate white spats, kilt and huge white sporran, proudly wearing his red hackle and tam-o'-shanter. All eyes were on him – a small, powerfully built man with a chestful of medals – as he barked orders at his men. In my final term, I got up the courage to speak to Sergeant Claus about my enduring dream of joining the other Jocks. I expected to be yelled at because I wanted to leave his regiment after they had spent a year training me. But he was very receptive, arranging for me to see Major Young. I explained to him that I was grateful for everything I had learned with the Staffs but had a strong calling to join the Black Watch.

Plenty of red tape followed and then a meeting with Sergeant Claus and Lieutenant Phipps. 'Are you sure you know what you're doing?' asked Phipps, who seemed to have forgiven me for his sore backside. 'You're not really a Jock – you've lived here too long. You should stick with us. You can have a great career in the Staffs.'

'Those guys do things differently to us,' added Claus.

'They're not very sympathetic if you're feeling under the weather. You won't be able to take a day off sick,' said Phipps. 'They're fucking savages.'

But nothing would dissuade me. My application was accepted and I was transferred on paper to the Black Watch.

The Junior Leaders' passing-out parade was in August 1984. I was put in charge of a platoon of 30 men, the last unit to march off the parade ground. We saluted the dais, watched by a large crowd of visiting relatives, including Mum, Bob and Uncle Robert. Then I rushed to meet my family, forgetting that I was carrying my SLR horizontally with its bayonet fixed. A corporal grabbed and bollocked me before I could stab my mum in the chest.

It was Mum's introduction to my army life and she met some of my instructors at the reception afterwards. We had known bleak times as a family but Mum had always been a fount of strength and encouragement. Now she could see her efforts paying off, as her elder boy became a qualified soldier with a promising future.

• • •

After two weeks' leave, I caught the train from Birmingham to Edinburgh. It was my first visit to the grand city. Full of excitement, I went to the Glencorse training depot, where I was to spend two months being inducted into the Black Watch. It turned out that there wasn't much to do except proudly collect my kilt, take more fitness and medical tests and attend indoctrination lectures about the history of the Black Watch and the regiment's ways of doing things (involving lots of parading and shouting).

I grew familiar with the challenges of the famous Black Watch regalia. There were several variants, such as 'review order', which was blue bonnet, red hackle, shirt and tie, brown jacket, kilt, sporran, black brogues and white spats. You had to look perfect and we learned to paint our spats with whitener while protecting their buttons with tinfoil.

Although we had been in different companies, I quickly bonded with the other graduates from Shorncliffe, especially Benny Wilson, Ian Sherriff, 'Dodger' and Cammy Laverty. After a couple of visits to the NAAFI club, we realised that we needed to stick together. The atmosphere was stunningly different from Shorncliffe's. Instead of having earnest chats about military life, soldiers could be seen staggering about, fighting each other and spewing threats in our direction. Several times at night, older guys tried to break into our room. Once when I was on guard duty with another guy, two drunks threatened us with a pickaxe handle because they wanted to sleep in our beds just off the guardroom, being too pissed and lazy to walk to their own.

It was like being back on the Durham Estate, where the law of the jungle prevailed – a cruel disappointment. Was this really the noble regiment? Glencorse must be an aberration, I decided. Some of the older guys were probably jealous of us because, as Junior Leaders, we were better trained than they were. I couldn't wait to get to Germany and, I hoped, some decent Scottish soldiering.

In November, we flew to RAF Gütersloh and then drove to the Black Watch barracks in Werl. It was almost deserted, with most of the Jocks away on a big exercise in Canada. But on our first night, we got another glimpse of the less savoury side of army life. A drunken gang broke into the juniors' room and attacked Benny Wilson, only backing off when he pulled a knife on them. They were led by a giant guy who had been put in charge of showing us around the base. Things got worse when everyone came back from Canada and the juniors were split up. The NAAFI club was best avoided unless you were looking for cheap booze and violence. The base seethed with tribal tensions between men from different Scottish towns such as Perth, Arbroath and Dundee. I kept quiet about my Brummie background. After my stellar performance at Shorncliffe, it was as if I had gone from hero to zero.

I was assigned to 6 Platoon in Bravo Company. We were led by a first-rate sergeant, Colin Gray, who has since become a good friend. One morning, he called me out on muster parade, held every morning at 0800 hours and something akin to a religious ceremony in the Black Watch. 'Henderson, come here!' I marched out, wondering what I had done wrong. 'Turn to face the platoon.' I about-turned. 'I am sick of men turning up on parade without starched shirt collars. Look at Henderson. I want you all to follow his example.' Then he praised my brightly bulled boots before ordering me to fall back beside men in their 20s who had just been told to emulate a 17 year old. They weren't happy and I was sent to Coventry for a while.

The company was dominated by a bullying clique led by two guys known as 'Jacko' and 'Spud', aided and abetted by some NCOs. I was shocked to learn that some of the older guys didn't even want to be soldiers. They were either serving out their contracts resentfully or couldn't think of anything better to do. For me, the army was a vocation and I just wanted to get on with honing my skills and advancing my career. There was an unwritten rule that a junior lad had to stand up whenever a senior came into the room. This was anathema to me. Why should I get up for someone of the same rank just because he was older? We all had the same chances and if they hadn't been promoted, it must be because they were lazy or not good enough. I spoke my mind to some of the lads and news of my defiance spread.

One afternoon, as I queued in the cookhouse, a stocky guy from Charlie Company suddenly came up and, without a word, head-butted me. I reeled in shock and, as a black eye ripened, weighed up my options. I was a good boxer now and familiar with martial arts but retaliating might cause me bother with the other men in Charlie Company. No doubt my attacker had been put up to it by Jacko's gang. I decided to swallow my pride for the time being.

A week later, Spud collared me. 'Time to learn some respect, ya cheeky cunt. You're gonnae get filled in later.' This was a declaration of war. That night, I planned to stay alert but drifted off to sleep. Then my eyes opened with the pain of a thump in the mouth. Jacko was straddling me. I reached under the bunk and smashed a red-hot iron that I'd kept plugged in into his face. He screamed like a dying beast and rolled onto the floor as I followed and punched him repeatedly. Then he was gone from the room, leaving behind splodges of blood and his front teeth.

For the rest of the night, I sat up talking to my new pals Stevie Anderson and 'Howling Mad' Murdoch, who was hairier than a wolf. 'I'm not sure I can take any more of this,' I kept saying. I felt my dream was going sour. But at least I had no more bother from Jacko.

THREE

Bandit Country

I was so disillusioned that I would have considered leaving the army if I hadn't been tied to it by a three-year contract. But then a sea change in B Company suddenly shifted the ground away from the bullies and skivers towards those who wanted to be professional soldiers. This coincided with the Black Watch's preparations for a posting to South Armagh in Northern Ireland. A new company commander, Nigel Lithgow, took over when we returned to Scotland in April 1984, based at Kirknewton, near Edinburgh. He was Black Watch born and bred – his father had been the regimental CO – and a hard taskmaster. He set a new tone, clamping down on drunkenness and devising an intensive training programme. We called him 'Let's Go Lithgow' because of his awesome enthusiasm.

Let's Go was complemented by a new sergeant major, Ramsey Macdonald, who was equally steeped in the best ways of the Black Watch. 'Rambo' was a barrel-chested giant, one of five brothers wearing the red hackle. 'If ye don't finish the run, I'll fill you in,' he'd joke. 'And if you're too fucking big, I'll get my brothers to fill you in.' He had four metal lockers in his office, all dented because sometimes he'd bounce you off them, one at a time. But he wasn't spiteful and would rarely put you on a charge for some minor misdemeanour. He was generous with his time and encouragement. His real boss was his wife, Maureen, whom he dearly loved. She drove him everywhere as, surprisingly, he didn't have a licence. He was someone I admired as a professional soldier and a good family man.

'Starchy' Smith – even his spats were starched – was the regimental sergeant major and another iconic figure. The bullies feared him and we hungry young professionals respected him. Every week, he took 500 men on regimental parade around Kirknewton airbase. It was an often windy mile-and-a-half trek, and woe betide anyone whose hat and hackle blew off! Jocks pulled their headgear tight over their ears and went around afterwards with red rings on their foreheads.

With Let's Go and Rambo in charge, I felt I could thrive in B Company's new meritocracy. We did lots of arduous runs and I was always out in front, as I had been at Shorncliffe. Sometimes we ran in four-man teams, carrying twenty-four-pound GPMGs and full kit over eight miles of rough terrain. We had to start and finish together. It was good preparation for operating in four-man patrol units in Northern Ireland.

In Edinburgh, I had my first taste of royal duties. Terry Donovan and I were chosen, because of our height and bearing, to provide the Queen's guard of honour when she came to stay at Holyrood Palace. Terry was a funny guy, especially when he smiled, because he had no front teeth. We did lots of rehearsals. As the Queen approached, we were meant to swing our heads and eyes towards her. But, perhaps through nerves, Terry forgot this and stared straight ahead. 'Psst!' I tried to catch his attention but the Queen looked round first. This happened before a parade of 200 men and we got a right bollocking, although we were allowed to carry on with our duties. At night, we had to replace our ceremonial brogues with trainers in case we disturbed Her Majesty's sleep.

One morning, Prince Philip came out with the dogs and I sprang to attention and presented arms. He ignored me but a corgi came over to piss on my leg. When I thought no one was looking, I broke ranks and surveyed the damage. I hate those fucking dogs, I thought. Suddenly, Phil the Greek was back. 'Sorry about that, old chap,' he said, as I jumped rigidly to attention again, one spat white and the other yellow.

• • •

Our base at Kirknewton was a grim collection of Nissen huts built for Canadian airmen in the Second World War. I was glad to get away one weekend and visit my family in Birmingham. I arrived home with my portable TV, a recent purchase that I was particularly proud of. I'd brought it with me on the train so I could watch it in my bedroom. We ordered a takeaway, rented a video and settled in for the night – me, Mum and Bob, who was now 14 and the man of the house.

There was a knock at the door and, as Mum got up, my sixth sense told me to expect trouble. 'Be quiet,' I heard her whisper. Then the sound of Terry's jabber chilled me. Wasn't that man out of our lives?

Painful memories flooded my thoughts as I followed Mum to the door. She was crying. Terry looked older. I was much taller than him now. One thing hadn't changed: he was still swaying with the drink. 'It's the tough soldier boy,' he jeered. And this from someone who, as a young man, had been locked up for desertion and dishonourably discharged. He couldn't hack the army but he could batter women and children.

I was boiling with anger but Mum restrained me. Then Terry grabbed at my arm. He's trying to control us again, I thought. Remembering how he had put Mum in hospital, I gently pushed her away from the door. 'Please get inside, Mum, and lock the door.' I shut the door and stepped out, catching Terry in a painful aikido armlock. The pig started squealing. I dragged him over to a wall, where he tripped and bashed his face. 'You made our lives hell,' I told him. 'Don't ever come back.'

I pushed him to the ground, where he crumpled pathetically. 'Don't be here when I look out the window,' I warned him, 'or you'll get more of the same.' It was the last time we ever saw him.

• • •

We started preparing for Northern Ireland 20 months in advance, practising ambushes in the winter snow at Werl. In the 1980s, unlike today, the army had the luxury of time to make long-term plans. Back in Britain, our training programme was coordinated by NITAT (the Northern Ireland Training Advisory Team). There were lots of lectures, with 500 of us sitting in cinemas listening to intelligence bods and officers from units currently serving in the province. The Black Watch had served in Belfast and there was talk about how South Armagh was a different, rural environment. It was a Provisional IRA stronghold, where they could attack us and easily slip across the border into the Republic of Ireland. In September 1984, the IRA almost succeeded in blowing up the Prime Minister, Margaret Thatcher. They were a serious threat. We were told that all the paramilitaries, both Catholic and Protestant, were knee-deep in protection rackets, drug running and other crime. Slides of the main IRA players in South Armagh featured 'Slab' Murphy. They told us that his farm straddled the border, with underground pipes for his oil-smuggling activities.

We would be combining army and policing roles and we studied map reading, the legality of stop-and-search and the 'yellow card' rules of engagement. These said that you must not open fire without issuing a warning unless you faced an immediate, direct threat. Our skills were sharpened in mock towns at army centres in Lydd and Hythe, near Folkestone. Soldiers back from Ireland would dress in civvies and play the part of rioting crowds or terrorists smashing cars through our checkpoints. For training in a rural environment, we went to the training area at Stanford, near Colchester, and lay in the rain for hours with listening devices. We were practising protecting 'soft targets' under threat from assassination, such as retired UDR (Ulster Defence Regiment) men.

I first met Mike Riddell-Webster, who would later lead us into Iraq, during training for Northern Ireland, on a course in signalling. He was then the commander of the signal platoon and introduced the course, talking about how good it could be for our careers. We tackled topics like the Morse code, high-frequency antenna lengths and message encryption. I found it fascinating, came top of the class and went proudly back to my platoon with a cup and a certificate. When at last we went to Northern Ireland, Let's Go chose me as his bodyguard and signaller. I accompanied him on patrols, carrying a GPMG, ready to protect the company commander at all costs. I also had a radio to transmit his messages in the accepted speech codes. Sometimes these dealt with critical troop movements. It was vital to get all the details right. At just 18, it was a great honour for me.

In November 1985, we flew out for a six-month tour of duty. The smell of aviation fuel stirred my adrenalin, sparking fearful anticipation. We were going to the area where the IRA had killed more British soldiers than anywhere else and B Company would be right on the front line, in the village of Crossmaglen. From Aldergrove airport, near Belfast, we flew to Bessbrook Mill, the British Army's HQ in South Armagh, to board Wessex and Chinook helicopters. Against the din of rotor blades, we ran past men from the Royal Regiment of Fusiliers who had just disembarked at the end of their tour of duty. 'Bad luck, lads,' they joked, with cheesy grins. 'Think of us sat in the pub next week!'

We were packed into the helicopters, where we fought for window space, keen for an early glimpse of 'bandit country'. It was cold with the gunner's door open as we flew over the Camlough Mountain and its hilltop military observation posts. As we approached Crossmaglen, I was struck by the peaceful green fields, stone walls and churches. Our base, however, was less idyllic. A grubby, depressing joint, it was so dirty that one soldier caught scabies. Even the dogs didn't like us there. Packs of them hung around the back gate and Ronnie 'Le Suave', who was tubby and slow, often came in from patrols with an Alsatian hanging off his arse.

We were there over the Christmas season and one day, while patrolling the village, I stopped at a manger to genuflect and make the sign of the cross. An old lady lambasted me. 'What the fuck are ye doin', ye Brit bastard? Taking the piss out of our Lord and his mother Mary?' I was very naive about politics and decided to read some Irish history. Learning how the Irish had suffered down the centuries made me sympathise with the republican cause. What would I do, I wondered, if someone invaded my country, my village? We were an occupying power and, especially as a Catholic, I never felt fully comfortable with our way of doing things. But I had no time for the IRA's terrorist methods and felt that their politics were often used as a cover for gang crime. If any of them were a direct threat to me or my men, I wouldn't hesitate to kill them.

On my 19th birthday, in February 1986, I took the radio report of our first bomb attack. 'Contact. 14 Delta. One man down, possibly dead. Wait. Out.' Let's Go, Sergeant Cross (our medic) and I dashed to the Monog Road, one of five main roads into the village. The bomb had been detonated as a foot patrol passed. Rubble was strewn around. 'Jeebers', the regimental police corporal, stood in the middle of the road covered in dust. His hair seemed to be smouldering.

Sergeant Cross ran up and touched his arm. 'Are you OK?' he asked.

'Get yer fucking hands off me!' roared Jeebers.

Even after dicing with death, the 'Horrible Bastard' lived up to his nickname.

Eddie Floan was unconscious and he was rushed to hospital by helicopter. Luckily, he survived, having received a broken jaw. The IRA had hidden the bomb too deep in the ground.

Two men from Delta Company had an even luckier escape when a bomb exploded at a gate between two stone pillars on a hilltop. Johnny McElvy had taken up a fire position to look over the brow and was blown into the air and onto the back of his commander, Lieutenant Ricky Dinsmore. I rushed there in a quick-support helicopter with our second in command, Captain Rupert Forrest. I was shocked by how powerful the blast had been. The pillars had been shattered into big lumps of stone, which were embedded in the ground, sometimes a foot deep, over a wide area. Somehow, Johnny lived to fight another day.

Because of my signals training, I did several stags at the operations room, encoding messages and manning the computer system codenamed 'Vengeful', which held records of every vehicle licensed on the province, including details of stolen cars and those owned by suspected terrorists. Soldiers out on patrol would request information and you had to be quick in responding because they might be holding a car at a checkpoint or asking about one that had just gone past. My personal standard was to have the data ready by the time the solider said 'over'. I took great pride in all of my work.

There was a disastrous breach of discipline one day when a corporal and some pals broke the 'two-can rule' on camp and had a few beers. They were watching the CCTV cameras and spotted a known player entering a chip shop in the village. They ran out pissed in their tracksuits and punctured the man's lung with a knife. There was a riot outside the camp the next day. One local got run over and another was nearly shot. Then the RUC came to make arrests and the corporal and another guy were jailed for assault. This lamentable incident reflected the soldiers' frustration that terrorists could attack and kill them with little fear of capture. I felt sorry for my commanders, Let's Go and Rambo, who were put unfairly in the spotlight.

A patrol unit struck another blow against community relations by pouring blue paint over a rising-phoenix statue. The villagers had clubbed together to pay for this republican monument and defacing it was a sure-fire way of completely alienating them. It reminded me that we were an overwhelmingly Protestant force in an overwhelmingly Catholic area. The Masonic Order had a lodge in our sergeants' mess, Red Hand of Ulster flags fluttered in our camp and, in the years to come, Jocks would join Orange Order marches in their civvies to play in the flute bands. I was one of a minority of Black Watch 'Fenian bastards'. While a few Jocks even went about defiantly in Celtic tops, some Catholics converted for an easier life. For me, though, that would have been a betrayal of my mother.

One serious incident could have been avoided. I knew the platoon sergeant involved and I didn't think much of his abilities. When his men were caught in a night-time ambush, I feared the worst. He had broken a cardinal rule by taking his platoon into a barn to sleep. They had been 'dicked' (spotted) and the IRA sent a seven-man team to a nearby hill to rain M60 and Armalite fire down on them. In what was the longest gun battle in the history of the Troubles, 2,000 rounds were exchanged. Incredibly, no one was hurt. The barn was riddled with bullets but fortunately the enemy's night-sights made them aim too high. We flew by helicopter to the scene, arriving just as the IRA had slipped away across the border.

The post-incident report made sorry reading. It turned out that one Jock had a powerful M79 grenade launcher strapped inside his Bergen backpack instead of slung over his shoulder ready to fire. Another man bravely stepped outside the barn but then fired across the entrance, trapping everyone else inside. Meanwhile, the platoon sergeant hid behind a cement mixer. He was reduced to corporal and removed from his company.

FOUR

Saved by the Hesh

A gang of us celebrated the end of the Northern Ireland tour on a Club 18–30 holiday in Magaluf. I hooked up with a girl called Nicola there after bumping into her when I stepped out of a hotel lift in a grass skirt. She lived in London and I wanted to see her again when we got home.

Back in Edinburgh, now at Redford Barracks, I went on a one-week intensive driving course with two of my mates. Our instructor was Sergeant Jock Todd, who seemed like a miserable old bastard even though he was still only in his 30s. His rigorous teaching methods included thumping your hand or leg with a black rubber hose if you upset him by touching the steering wheel too soon or pressing too hard on the accelerator. When Billy 'Basher' Sexton took his turn in the driving seat, Stevie Anderson and I sat in the back determined that he would get a good whacking. We took the brown-paper bags that we'd collected with our food from the cookhouse and pulled them tightly over our faces, with holes torn in them for our eyes. Every time Basher looked in the mirror he burst out laughing at the two Freddy Kruegers in the back. 'What's so fucking funny?' raged Todd, as he wielded the rubber hose.

Despite these antics, we passed the test on the Friday and immediately hired a car to drive down to London, where I had a good time with Nicola. On the Sunday night, I arrived back at the barracks, relaxed in my civvies and wearing no socks with my shoes. The guardroom was manned by Willie Dixon, the regimental police sergeant. We called him 'Willie Wessex', after the helicopters, because he was always getting into a flap. He stuck his head out the hatch window, like the gatekeeper in *The Wizard of Oz*. It had been a fine summer's day and the sun had left its mark on him.

'What's up with your nose, Sergeant?' I asked, with an incautious giggle.

'I'll tell you what's up with my nose, ya numpty,' he fumed. 'Aren't you a bit warm yourself, with no fucking socks on? You'd better come in the back and cool off.'

He then treated me to my first taste of army jail, where Corporal Jeebers came to see me. He was five feet tall and as wide, with no neck. He introduced me to Big Bertha, a huge machine for shining wooden floors. Jeebers beasted me all over the jail with her.

'Right, ya prick, when I say "BLACK", Bertha goes forward. And when I say "WATCH", Bertha goes back. You got that, ya maggot?'

'Yes, Corporal.'

He then screamed rapidly: 'BLACK WATCH, BLACK WATCH, BLACK WATCH, BLACK WATCH!'

The sweat dripped off of me but I wouldn't give up, so he made me try to bump the ceiling.

I was formally charged and later marched in front of the major, who would, I felt sure, throw the case out. 'Are you 24683084 Private Henderson?' he asked. 'You are formally charged with being incorrectly dressed by wearing no socks with your civilian clothes.' I stood there fuming, waiting for a clown to jump out of the cupboard. There was nothing in the rules about what you wore off duty. But I pleaded guilty and was fined £20. The Black Watch regime could be irritatingly arbitrary.

• • •

In the winter of 1986, I was posted to West Berlin, the epicentre of the Cold War, in the middle of East German territory. There was no sign of the winds of change that would soon topple the

Soviet Union, demolish the Berlin Wall and reunify Germany. Indeed, the atmosphere was feverish. 'If the Soviets attack, your life expectancy is three minutes,' we were told. We were based at the Montgomery Barracks, on the border. If we looked through the high fence at the back of the camp, we could see East German guards with fierce dogs running about on very long ropes and tanks and artillery pointed at us.

We did FIBUA training at Ruhleben, a military mock town in a suburb of West Berlin. FIBUA stands for 'fighting in built-up areas', sometimes referred to as 'conventional warfare in an urban environment'. We practised fighting from supermarkets, shoring up buildings hit by artillery, laying down sniper positions and setting up anti-tank missile posts. We studied the lessons of the Red Army's capture of the Reichstag in 1945. It had taken several thousand men in the face of intense pockets of Nazi resistance.

When we weren't on duty, downtown Berlin beckoned. With its lively bars and discos, legalised prostitution and porno shops as brazen as McDonald's outlets, it was a magnet for young men. Perhaps in response to my £20 fine, I made a habit now of wearing my regimental tie and a blazer everywhere. A gang of us would hit town regularly in the same attire. We drank lots of beer and enjoyed ourselves but there were also many fights with groups of knife-carrying Turks.

• • •

By now, I'd been transferred to C Company, along with about a dozen of the more experienced soldiers from B Company. It was the start of my long association with Charlie Company, its members known in the regiment as 'the Savages' for their legendary brawling. They were a company of weapons specialists, including an anti-tank platoon who used the Milan missile system, a mortar platoon and a recce platoon with the latest surveillance gear. You had to spend time in a duty company before you could join the Savages and it contained a lot of older men, including privates in their 30s who had specialist skills.

The company was run at that time by an unforgettable duo. Our sergeant major was Willie Boyle, the man whose parade skills had entranced me back at Shorncliffe. He was short and powerfully built. We called him 'Barney Rubble' and chuckled at his distinctive nasal twang.

'What's the fucking score here?' he'd moan if you came back to camp late or committed some other misdemeanour.

'The bus broke down, sir,' you might say.

'Pish, knickers, shite! And you are in the shite!' he'd rage.

'My arse!' was Barney's catchphrase long before Ricky Tomlinson used it on *The Royle Family*.

Our company commander, Major Johnny Monteith, was a tall man, about six foot four, and bald apart from some fluff that he liked to grow around the sides of his head until it flapped in the wind. When he wasn't on his bike, he ran about in a noisy old VW, with the exhaust pipe held in place with elastic bands. His natural gait was a lurch rather than a walk, his torso on the brink of toppling as his legs caught up, his arms held out like he was carrying a couple of TVs. He wasn't the type of man to play the tough guy. Our beloved commander was better known to us as 'the Hesh' (high-explosive squash heid).

Once, when I was on guard duty, the Hesh waltzed up to the security barrier pushing his bike. 'Don't worry, Henderson, I can duck under the barrier,' he said, forgetting about the small child perched on the back of the bike.

On an icy day, he fell off his bike at a speed bump, toppling over in his kilt. 'Don't any of you fucking laugh or you're in the jail,' Barney muttered to a group of us who were enjoying the show. Then the Hesh was up and off as if nothing had happened. 'Right, is he away?' asked Barney. 'You've got one minute to laugh.'

Another morning, the Hesh arrived to inspect our kit and anti-tank vehicles in near-full kilt drill order. He was wearing his kilt, green jumper, tam-o'-shanter and red hackle. But, instead of regimental brogues and green socks, he sported flip-flops and bandaged feet, after the result of a mountaineering trip.

The Hesh often got me to drive him places and one day, after an exercise, I took him to catch a plane to a family wedding. As we sped along, he pulled a crumpled suit from the bottom of his pack and climbed into the back of the Land Rover to change. When we arrived, he thanked me and strode off for his plane wearing green army socks, his face still black with camouflage paint.

He showed an unconventional approach to discipline. I was queuing outside his office with several others, all of us on some minor charge. The standard procedure was for the sergeant major to march you into the company commander's office and march you out after your hearing. But that day the Hesh was in a hurry.

'Listen, you reprobates, I haven't got time to wait for the sergeant major and so I am going to be him. Henderson, you're in first and once I've found you guilty, you can march the others in. OK. Left, right, left, right, left, right, halt, about-turn!'

He left me facing his desk while he ran through the door behind me into the sergeant major's office and out into the corridor, then walked back into his office, sat down, found me guilty of incorrect parking and issued a small fine. Then he went out of the room and back through the sergeant major's office to march me out.

'OK, your turn now, Henderson.'

I marched them in, one at a time, until Barney Rubble appeared.

'What the fuck's going on here?'

'The company commander was playing sergeant major, sir.'

'What the fuck? He can't do that!'

He strode in and we listened to an entertaining argument.

'Well, I was in a hurry. They've all been found guilty,' insisted the Hesh.

I don't think Barney ever deducted the fines from our wages.

Another time, in the Hesh's car, he spoke to me about a charge I faced for fighting. 'How much money have you got this month, Henderson?' he asked.

'I'm a bit skint, sir.'

'Well, how about if I fine you 50 Deutschmarks. How does that sound?'

'That would be very good, thank you, sir,' I replied with relief.

I knew something was up when I appeared before him with Barney Rubble at my side.

'I am fining you 100 Deutschmarks. Right, Sergeant Major, march him out!'

He wanted me gone quickly but I couldn't contain myself. 'But you said 50 Deutschmarks!'

'What the fuck?' muttered Barney as he shut the door. 'Fine by negotiation!'

For the next three days, I refused to speak to the Hesh, even when I drove him about. Then the Land Rover we were in broke down and he went to check the oil, wiping the dipstick with his tam-o'-shanter which he then put back on his head. I burst out laughing.

'What's the problem, Henderson? You've been very quiet.'

'You fined me 100 Deutschmarks after promising me 50.'

'Ah, yes, but the CO spoke to me and said it was a serious offence and the fine must reflect this. He was talking about putting you in jail.'

As usual, the Hesh's motives were irreproachable.

• • •

One of our tasks on that tour was guarding Spandau Prison. For 20 years, it had held just one prisoner: Rudolf Hess. He had been Hitler's deputy until, in 1941, he made a mysterious flight to Scotland, perhaps aiming to negotiate peace with Britain. He was captured and at the Nuremberg trials he was sentenced to life imprisonment at Spandau. Under an agreement reached then, the prison was guarded in a monthly rotation by Berlin's four occupying powers: Britain, the USA, France and the Soviet Union. This gave the Russians a good excuse to sniff around West Berlin. They gave Hess a hard time when they were in charge, removing his video and TV. As the Communist Party newspaper *Pravda* put it: 'The conscience of the people dictates that the Hitlerite lieutenant Hess must drink his retribution to the bottom of the cup.'

In his 90s, Hess cut a pathetic figure, pinch-faced and hunched, shuffling from his cell to a shed in the prison garden, where he sat most days wearing an oxygen mask. He would always try to speak to us. We were under strict instructions not to respond. One day, he managed to persuade a Jock to throw him a cigarette and then reported the soldier to his guard. The guy got 28 days in jail. The old Nazi still had a nasty streak.

In August 1987, Hess was found dead with a length of electrical cord around his neck. His death was recorded as suicide. We were relieved that it had happened while the prison was in American hands. We had been briefed that if it had been in Soviet hands when Hess had died, the Russians would have put a museum on the site as an excuse for maintaining a presence there. We kept guarding the prison, keeping away the neo-Nazis who wanted to turn it into a shrine, and I had a good look around just before it was demolished. Toby Styles and I were among the last people inside Hess's cell, which was spacious, with lots of modern electrical fittings and a porcelain sink.

In the rest of the prison, we made some gruesome finds. The basement held stone cells so small that you could put your arms out and touch opposite walls. The cells contained small metal cages. I tried to imagine the horror of being squashed inside a cage within a cell. One cell wall had a roughly etched calendar, marking the days of 1942, 1943 and 1944. Outside, an execution wall was pitted with bullet holes. Back inside, there was a furnace linked to a big chimney, and a macabre kind of operating theatre with a central stone table and guttering in the floor, as if to drain away blood and fluids. The place oozed inhumanity. I was glad when it was bulldozed to the ground. In order to thwart the memorabilia hunters, the rubble was crushed in a quarry and dumped in the North Sea and a NAAFI was built on the site.

• • •

With the notorious wall, a heavy military presence and the sense that spies were everywhere, Berlin worked on my imagination. It sometimes felt like being on the set of an espionage movie. When girls got friendly in the downtown clubs, I found myself wondering if they were working for the Stasi.

Sometimes we travelled by train through East Germany to do training in West Germany. We covered any tanks or artillery attached to our train and were meant to take notes if we spotted East German or Red Army gear. Photography was strictly forbidden. But despite the cloak-and-dagger atmosphere, our guys often swapped badges with 'enemy' troops if they were lined up on the platform as we pulled into a station.

We were allowed recreational trips to East Berlin. While Mercedes glided through West Berlin, the emblem of the East was a battered old Trabant. Across the wall, the Deutschmark was valued at 10 times the East German mark and they seemed happy to take our money. We dined in the poshest restaurants and bought luxuries for pennies.

Ten of us made one trip intent on mischief. We settled in for the afternoon at a Turkish restaurant, where we ate caviar and drank copious amounts of champagne while wearing the big furry hats that we had just bought and calling each other Brezhnev. The waiters were amused at first but got edgy when Jocks started doing the Soviet goosestep. We were told to leave as they called the police and we drove back to Checkpoint Charlie.

The procedure on the eastern side was that you had to hold your ID card up and face the window while an East German or Russian soldier eyeballed you before waving you through. This time, Stevie Trotter decided to pin his card to the window with his bare arse – the biggest I have ever seen. The East Germans reported us and, back at our barracks, we were thrown in jail for the night. The NCOs among us were reduced to the ranks, an experience with which I was to become all too familiar.

• • •

In July 1987, our CO, Lieutenant Colonel Alistair Irwin (who would become the British Army's adjutant general), promoted me to lance corporal, the youngest in the Black Watch at the time. Before my promotion came a fantastic eight-week course covering discipline, fitness and leadership, in which I was placed third overall and top at drill. It was a huge honour for me to lead the parade of the new NCOs in front of the whole regiment.

Life was good, although clouded by bullying. Some of the old hands resented the upwardly mobile young Jocks who'd recently joined from Bravo Company. Ever since my showdown with Jacko, I'd stuck by a rule that if anyone hit me I would fight back.

One night, I had a group of mates in my room, laughing and watching TV, when we were rudely interrupted by two guys, both drunk, who grabbed my friend David Eason and started pushing him about. Eventually I persuaded them to go but I couldn't sleep that night. This can't happen again, I resolved.

A week later, they were back. This time, I grabbed one and smashed his head against the wall. The other fled to his room but I followed him and banged on the door until he opened it. 'It ends tonight,' I told him. 'Any more, and me and my friends will be coming for you.' I was charged with fighting and reduced to the ranks. It was a devastating blow but at least I'd gained kudos as a guy who took no shit and this encouraged more young Jocks to resist the bullying culture.

Scrapping was routine in the Black Watch but especially in Germany, where we were permanently hyped for a war that never happened. The NAAFI bar was a tense place; every company had its space and every man his seat. Once I was at the bar when an old hand asked me out for a fight. I obliged and was taken aback when he tried to smack me around the head with a fire extinguisher. After I'd wrestled it from him and knocked him out, I combed my hair and went back to finish my pint.

After being 'bust' to the ranks, I kept my nose clean for several months and was delighted to be promoted back to lance corporal. Then I broke my leg representing Charlie Company in an athletics competition and spent two weeks in traction at the Berlin Military Hospital. On my ward there were two young men from the King's Own Scottish Borderers who had a shocking tale. As part of an initiation ritual, they had been tied up in mattress covers and thrown out of a high window. They were lucky to have got away with several broken limbs. Stories of brutality in the regiment hit the headlines and the CO and RSM (regimental sergeant major) were both kicked out of the army. Meeting these lads was depressing. It made me wonder if anything could be done about the endemic bullying. I can say now that I'm proud to have stood up and challenged it.

I came out of hospital on crutches and then almost had to wave my career goodbye. Three of us went for some beers downtown and were heading across a busy road for a McDonald's when a car full of Turks careered across the street and clipped Rab Penman. He grabbed the open window to steady himself and they all jumped out wielding knives. Rab was slashed across the stomach and I found myself facing a guy with a shiny blade. I pulled the rubber end off a crutch and whacked the Turk on the forehead, leaving a circular imprint. We regrouped in McDonald's but had to bomb-burst through a door when an even bigger group of Turks gathered outside. The Jocks were in full retreat and I was doing my best to keep up. Then someone grabbed me and I spun around to confront a West German police officer.

It was back to the bed blocks. I spent two weeks in the army jail and was hauled in front of the Black Watch's commanding officer. The police had sent a damning report and this was seen as too big an offence for the Hesh to deal with. It was a grievous blow when I was ordered to hand back my brassard.

There was a quirky side to the proceedings. Three weeks earlier, on guard duty as lance corporal, I had stopped a guy racing his car on camp. After being bust for the second time, I had to go straight back in front of the CO and give evidence against the soldier who I had charged with drink-driving. 'Well done, Henderson. Commendable vigilance,' said the CO, minutes after lambasting me for bringing the regiment into disrepute.

It felt like my army life was over. That evening, I walked to the car park, planning to go for a quiet spin. I needed to think about the rest of my life. I walked past the Hesh's office where, stark bollocknaked, he was getting changed with the lights on. He banged on the window and told me to come and speak to him.

'I've heard that you're thinking of leaving the army,' he said.

'Aye, sir, my three years are up next year and I'm thinking it'll be time to move on.'

I talked about my clashes with the bullies, how I'd just been defending myself against the Turks and how, as an adopted Catholic brought up in Birmingham, I felt an outsider even in the Black Watch. The Hesh produced a bottle of whisky. It was my first taste of the stuff and we spent hours talking. Through the fog of the malt, I received a clear message from him: 'I know you hate the bullies but you need to stay and make a difference.' It was a defining moment. I agreed and the Hesh would go on to repay me handsomely for my hard work.

He was always very supportive and I appreciated his kindness. One evening, he called for me with a spare ticket for a Michael Jackson concert at the Reichstag. I was thrilled to join him, his wife and Mike Riddell-Webster, who had risen to the rank of captain. As I got into the car, Riddell-Webster seemed less thrilled to see me. 'What's Henderson doing here?' he asked.

'Look, Henderson is one of my Jocks and I've invited him,' the Hesh replied.

In August 1989, we ended the tour with a talk by the Hesh in a cinema. I was nodding off at the back when he took me by surprise.

'Can Lance Corporal Henderson come to the stage?'

'How many times do I have to tell you, sir?' I protested to laughter. 'I'm not a lance corporal.'

'I'll tell you who is and who isn't,' he replied.

I went up for my third promotion to the same rank. This was almost unheard of and I was determined never to look back again.

FIVE

Upwardly Mobile

In the autumn of 1989, we were back in Northern Ireland for a varied two-year tour of duty. Based at the Ballykinlar base in County Down, which looked out onto the beach, we were deployed across the province, supporting other regiments in a mixture of urban and rural operations. Shortly after our arrival, I met a local nurse called Sharon. I thought she was fantastic and we were soon going steady.

In the new year, I won a place on the Section Commanders' Battle Course, also known as 'Junior Brecon'. It involved rigorous weapons training followed by six weeks at the Infantry Battle School in Brecon, where we spent most of our time on the Welsh mountains, going without sleep for days and honing our skills against a team of very experienced Gurkha troops. We were monitored to see if we could keep command of troops while being pushed to the limit of endurance. Our instructor was a tough paratrooper and several people dropped out. Even before I passed, Barney Rubble called me with the news that I had been promoted to full corporal.

Back in Ireland, I became a ground-team commander of a unit of four men (all Catholics, coincidentally) and second in command of a multiple (three units) of twelve men. We were in 9 Platoon and Stevie McDougall was our sergeant.

In Belfast, we did stints on guard duty at Crumlin Road jail. The level of violence there was shocking. We often saw loyalist prisoners dragging their own men to the toilets for savage punishment beatings. But we were ordered not to intervene – our job was just to reinforce the RUC and be ready to quell riots and stop breakouts. Shift changeovers involved walking through a 100-metre passage covered only with corrugated iron to the fortified position known as Sangar 10. This could be lively when the IRA decided to spray the passage with bullets. In the jail, I saw the men convicted of murdering corporals David Howes and Derek Wood in 1988. The corporals had been dragged from their car, beaten and shot dead after they blundered into the middle of an IRA funeral cortège. When I eyeballed one of the prisoners in his cell, he smirked back at me.

The corporals' terrible fate came back to me on an operation in South Armagh. We were to fly in by helicopter and I was told that there was a high risk of a surface-to-air missile attack. My unit would be the bait. Another helicopter would come to our aid if we were attacked. Fuck this, I thought, if I tell my Jocks, they'll all go sick. When we were airborne, with the gunner's door open, my eyes were peeled for signs of activity below. In the end, we swooped down safely and set up a VCP (vehicle checkpoint).

After a quiet time stopping cars and radioing information through to the Vengeful computer system, we began to make our way to an agreed rendezvous point where we would meet the other two units in our multiple. It was night-time and we cut across fields using a compass and electricity pylons as our guides. But my compass had no locking mechanism and I must have knocked its settings when we waded through a river, because it then took me to the wrong pylon. Soon, the four of us were on the outskirts of the village of Creggan, which was full of hardcore republicans. Dogs barked and doors opened. 'What are ye doin', ye Brit bastards? Ye'd best fuck off out of here!'

'Good evening to you, madam,' I replied, considering our options. We could run for it – and risk being followed by men with Armalites – or we could put on a front and make the locals think we were part of a larger team. I told my men to set up a VCP and check cars going in and out of the village. The Provos knew how we were meant to do things and would assume that our other units were within reach rather than several miles away. We kept up this façade while I got my bearings and eventually we headed to safety. I never told my men that we had got lost and after that I always carried two maps and two compasses.

Days later, we almost ran into a big republican funeral cortège thought to include the notorious 'Slab' Murphy. We kept to the fields until we reached a junction where I went down a road leading away from the cortège's route. I advanced 500 yards and knelt down in a fire position, waiting for my men to join me. Minutes passed but there was no sign of Ivor Devlin, who was meant to be the next down the road. Car engines were humming in the darkness.

'Ivor,' I whispered. 'Ivor. IVOR!' I lost it and yelled out loud before running back to the junction to see the now-dimming lights of the IRA's cars. Three white faces came out of the bushes. 'We thought you'd been put in the coffin,' one said. They hadn't heard me say where I was going.

We stuck together like penguins after that. It was an interesting return to bandit country. We weren't shot out of the sky and we didn't catch terrorists. But I caught a cold and learned some valuable lessons as a commander.

My first contact with the IRA came when they bombed a police car in the centre of Newry. People had thrown 'javelins' (tin cans packed with explosives and attached to a piece of broom handle) from the stairwell of some flats beside the Tall Man pub. Two exploded on impact and I tripped on a third running to the shattered car. We radioed for an ambulance for the injured police and set off in hot pursuit of the bombers. I ran up the stairs and along the balcony of the flats until I saw what looked like a handheld radio. Or was it an explosive device left behind to kill us? Fuck it, I thought – and not for the last time – it's 50–50. I ran on safely. The bombers got away, although the police caught up with them eventually.

I had a good memory for names and faces and a growing appetite for intelligence work. This was fuelled by several stints as the CONCO (continuity NCO) at Newry's Corry Square police station. Mostly, I liaised with Special Branch, ensuring that we could assist with their surveillance work and arrests. Through the job, I got information on all the town's known players and made an A-Z list in a notebook that I referred to on stop-and-searches and at VCPs. 'Good morning, Patrick,' I might say to unsettle a man listed in my book. 'Have you still got your membership of the IPLO [Irish People's Liberation Organisation]?'

Usually, I was polite and professional, even when dealing with known killers. One day, we stopped the Newry IRA boss at a VCP with his mum, gran and auntie. I knew he'd been searched earlier in the day and would have nothing on him while out with his family. There was no point in riling the women by making them get out to have their handbags searched. Instead, I chatted to the mum, leaving the IRA boss bemused at the wheel.

'Have you got any Kalashnikovs, Armalites or grenades in the boot?' I asked her.

'Just a couple of hundred,' she replied, 'but we're selling them up in Hilltown.'

'Oh well, so long as you'll not be using them against us.'

'Don't you worry,' she said, playing the part. 'And I hope it doesn't rain for you boys.'

Another stop-and-search conversation was more poignant. We stopped a man in the street and I did a 'Charlie One', contacting our base with his details. Back came the news that this was a brother of Mairead Farrell, one of three IRA members killed by the SAS on Gibraltar in 1988. They had been planning to bomb a changing-of-the-guard ceremony and were controversially shot dead in the street. The brother had a quiet, intelligent look. I spoke to him about the recent Old Firm game, in which Celtic had beaten Rangers, but he said he preferred hurling.

'Are you still pissed off about your sister?' I asked directly.

'Have you got family?' he replied. 'How would you feel if your sister or brother was murdered?'

'I understand what you're saying, especially if you think she was murdered,' I answered. 'But I couldn't condone a car bombing that would have killed innocent tourists. When we sign up to the army we accept that we might get killed in the line of duty. Surely it's the same when you take your oath of allegiance?'

He paused for a moment and then said, 'But that doesn't make the loss of a loved one any easier.'

I couldn't argue with him. But it angered all the British soldiers that known IRA leaders waltzed about their daily business, mostly undisturbed, while planning to bomb or shoot us at the first opportunity. This led to acts born of frustration, like the time a couple of Jocks hired a car with the avowed aim of running over a well-known player and Sinn Fein councillor who had poured a bucket of water over a comrade who'd called at his house. More seriously, I became aware that a man from the Royal Scots regiment had been caught passing documents with information about republicans to loyalist death squads. The soldier was given a suspended sentence by a military court and the army tightened up on access to confidential intelligence.

One day, 'Rambo', the Hilltown IRA commander, took me completely by surprise. We were on foot patrol outside the town when a man on a bike raced up behind me. As he passed me, he yelled so loudly that I jumped into the hedge. Then I saw Rambo twisting around to give me the finger as he sped downhill. I decided I was going to have the bastard and put the word out on the radio. An hour later, my colleague Jimmy Russell called from a checkpoint in the high street. 'We've got someone of interest to you,' he said. I arrived to find Rambo sitting in the cab of a coal truck. The Provos had access to all kinds of vehicles.

'Where's your bike?' I asked.

He looked at me and then burst out laughing. 'Aye, ye shat yourself, didn't ye?'

'Not as much as you will,' I replied, 'after we've kept you here all day.'

Rambo refused to leave the truck and I ordered Jojo McGuinness to drag him out. Rambo's shoes and socks came off in the struggle and Jojo ended up biting his toes. I think Rambo and I both had our fun that day.

When a couple of Jocks had their noses broken in rioting at Warrenpoint, South Down, we opted for an unconventional response. Two teams left their weapons and body armour in the police station and hid in alleyways carrying batons. Another team of uniformed soldiers went back into the street as bait and when the rioters returned (with their sticks, stones and iron bars) we all rushed out and gave them a good hiding.

It was a funnier day when I stopped the comedian Frank Carson at a border checkpoint.

'How ya doin'? What's the crack, Jock?' he asked me.

'Well, I'd like you to crack us a joke over the army radio.'

He was happy to oblige. I can't remember it but the gist was that he and his mum kept a roll of toilet paper in the living room because there was so much crap on the TV.

'It's the way I tell 'em!' he signed off, as always, with the whole of Charlie Company listening in. When I got back to base, Barney Rubble tried to kick me in the balls.

After Ireland, I was posted to Tern Hill Barracks in Shropshire, which had recently been bombed by the IRA. Then I went back to the Glencorse training depot, where I had begun my Black Watch career. I became a training corporal, putting new recruits through tough six-month courses before we handed them back to their regiments ready to go to war. In 1993, Sharon and I wed and moved into married quarters. It was a settled, happy time.

• • •

One day, an admin worker at Glencorse told me that I could use the serial number on my adoption certificate to find my birth certificate. This sparked my search for my birth mother. I had often wondered about my mother and father. Who were they? I knew only what the social worker had found out for me when I was 12. I decided the birth certificate might give me some clues.

I went to the General Register Office in Edinburgh with a friend.

After a long wait, a woman came back to the counter. 'Found it!' She handed me a pristine birth certificate recording the birth of Philip Gerard McKeown. I read the name slowly, torn between curiosity and alienation. Surely I was Tam, not Philip? Then I saw my birth mum's name – Anne McKeown. I stared at the signature. I was holding a trace of the woman who had brought me into the world. She was real.

The kind lady behind the counter spent ages searching for Anne's birth certificate but it wasn't there. I made an appointment with the Airdrie Court, which had handled my adoption. I felt nervous returning so near to where I'd spent my first years with Jessie and Pat Henderson. A clerk took me down to a room in the basement. 'You can make notes but please don't take any photographs,' she said, handing me a bundle of papers sealed with red wax, like something from the Middle Ages. I learned more about Anne McKeown. A short report of her troubled childhood said she had been born in Ireland, deserted by her mother (who ran off with a soldier when the family moved to Scotland) and put in the care of the Nazarene nuns. She had been persuaded by relations to give me up for adoption because she was not married.

The paperwork mentioned the St Margaret's Adoption Society and this was my next port of call. 'She went to London and we lost all trace of her,' I was told. 'If we hear anything, we'll let you know. But it's very unlikely.' Next, I called at Stobhill Hospital, cited on the certificate as my place of birth. The maternity ward had been closed down, however, and they didn't know where the records were.

For six months, I got on with my life, sad that I seemed to have reached a dead end. Then I got an electrifying letter from the adoption society. They had information for me. Would I come to see them? Soon, Sharon and I were back at their office, where we learned that Anne McKeown had written to the society, sending them a letter to give to me if I ever got in touch. 'You can read it now,' said the woman from the society. 'But we strongly advise you to think carefully about what you do next. We have contact officers who can help you to do things gradually.' I wasn't really listening.

We went to a private room where I slowly read the letter aloud to Sharon.

Dear Philip,

You may never get this letter but I'm your mother. I want to tell you how much I love you and how much I have thought about you every day since I lost you. I am hoping that before I die you will read this letter and one day I will see you again . . .

Anne continued for several pages, explaining more about her childhood, how cruel the nuns had been to her and how, as an unmarried teenager, she had given me up only under intense duress. She had come back from London for me but had been sent away. She asked me to forgive her. She was married now, with another two sons and a daughter. Her life was as happy as it could be but she would never be content until she found me. Sharon and I were sobbing. It was a painfully sad letter, laden with guilt. And it stirred strange feelings, knowing that I had another, mystery family.

Back home, I sat reading the letter repeatedly. 'I know what you're thinking but don't do it,' said Sharon, worried for me, as she went up to bed. I picked up the phone and dialled the number at the top of the letter. A man with a warm Glaswegian accent answered.

'Hello, this is Thomas Henderson. You might not know about me but I am Anne's son and I've just had a letter from her. Would you mind if I speak to her?'

'We've been looking for you for so many years,' said the man, introducing himself as Anne's husband Stewart. 'It is so good to hear from you. Would you mind giving me a few minutes to speak to Anne, because it'll be a shock to her and she'll be emotional, and then we'll call you back?'

The phone sat stubbornly quiet for a few minutes. Then it rang and I grabbed it.

'Hello, is that Philip?' It was a gentle voice.

'Yes.'

She started crying.

We talked for ages but I can remember almost nothing of the conversation. And we kept talking, exchanging letters and making calls, over many months.

When I was briefly based in Surrey, we met at last in a restaurant in Pirbright. Anne kept looking at me and touching me as our food lay almost untouched. And I kept staring at her, absorbing her features and mannerisms, noticing the ways in which we were alike. We drank some wine and giggled nervously. I felt she and her husband were like a couple about to take a new baby home from hospital. Stewart, a thoroughly decent man, told me the story of their fruitless trip back to Glasgow in 1967. Now they had found me and they were proud of my achievements with the Black Watch. Our relationship blossomed and I got to meet the rest of my second family, my brothers Gary and Stewart and my sister Angela. They were all extremely welcoming towards me from the start.

It was a while before I told my mum Jessie. But I always want her to know how much I love her and value everything that she has done for Bob and me. It's great to have the chance to say it here in print, for everyone to see.

• • •

As a soldier, I craved action. The Gulf War passed our regiment by and Northern Ireland was the only place where I could confront a real enemy, come face to face with killers and get the better of them. Having discovered an aptitude for intelligence work, I was pleased to get onto the selection for special forces.

The training was run by 14 Intelligence Unit, mostly at a camp in Shropshire. I was issued with a false ID card and referred to always as 'Number 155'. We were preparing to be undercover agents in a dangerous environment, learning high-speed driving skills and how to evade illegal checkpoints, break into houses and handle informants. There was a lot of role playing in the local towns and villages – following targets, meeting 'touts' in pubs and learning how best to cultivate them and glean useful information from them. The physical training – with sleep deprivation thrown in – was arduous but I was looking forward to a two-year tour as a special-forces operator. Then I was rushed to hospital after snapping my ankle during a log race. It was a bitter blow.

After I recovered, they wrote inviting me to finish the course. But Ed Jones, the Black Watch adjutant, persuaded me to make the Platoon Sergeants' Battle Course – 'Senior Brecon' – a priority instead. You had to pass this to become a fighting infantry sergeant. 'Best do it now,' he said, 'while you're 26 and at a peak of fitness.'

Junior Brecon trained you to lead 12 men; Senior Brecon prepared you to command 30. I got a commendation in the weapons training and made my second trip to the Welsh mountains. Once again, we spent days at a time living on rations and sleeping in little trenches covered with basha sheets while hiding from 'enemy' Gurkhas. But it was even more gruelling this time. Exercises included the 'Dragon Run': eight miles in full kit, followed by wading across a river and attacking targets.

I worked closely with several SAS guys, including a giant Fijian called 'Tokyo' and the man who has been immortalised in book and film as 'Stan'. Stan and I were paired off to dig a 'Milan trench', big enough to hold an anti-tank missile system. Exhausted in the early hours of the morning, we lit a small fire in the bottom of the trench and chatted.

'Have you heard of Andy McNab?' he asked.

'Is that Spike – Spike McNab?' I asked, thinking of someone in the KOSB.

'No!' he laughed. 'Andy McNab who's written that book *Bravo Two Zero*.'

Stan told me how, after Saddam invaded Kuwait in 1990, he had been part of an ill-fated SAS team operating undercover in Iraq. Some of them had died and others, including Stan, were captured and severely tortured. Stan was unhappy with McNab's bestselling book because, he said, it didn't tell the full story, including who had best stood up to interrogation.

The final Senior Brecon challenge was Pen y Fan, an 886-metre peak that we had to run over at speed as a team. I ended up carrying one guy's kit because he was almost collapsing, covered in snot. Another man fell off a cliff and was helicoptered to hospital.

When I passed, the instructor said I should go on selection for the SAS. I'd been given the same message after Junior Brecon. But I decided to set my sights elsewhere. Most of the best guys in the Black Watch – the likes of Stevie McDougall and Colin Gray – had qualified as Sandhurst instructors. This would be my next big challenge.

In 1994, I went back to Northern Ireland again as the 6 Platoon sergeant, based at Fort Whiterock in West Belfast. A ragged peace process was under way but we had a big riot on our hands following the release of Lee Clegg, a soldier accused of shooting dead two joyriders.

My regiment's sectarian hue shone through when we were visited by Patrick Mayhew MP, Secretary of State for Northern Ireland, and a representative of a women's group that we all dismissed as a front for Sinn Fein. They went around introducing themselves until they bumped into my sergeant major, who had a special fondness for King Billy.

'Hello,' said the woman, 'I'm Fionulla, from the West Belfast Women's Association.'

'And I'm commander of the Fort Whiterock UDF,' responded the sergeant major.

The minister almost dropped his tea and they both left in a hurry.

'What's the problem?' he wondered. 'I was just havin' the crack.'

Back in Scotland in 1995, I became the Black Watch recruitment sergeant for Dunfermline. Sharon and I bought a house on the banks of the Forth. It was a good time, personally and professionally. There was lots of work with schools and the local community, and I cultivated a new passion, becoming an army diving instructor. I also started running the 14 miles to and from my office, preparing for the coming Sandhurst challenge.

Six

Sandhurst Glory and a Funeral

The Royal Military Academy Sandhurst exuded imperial grandeur. A statue of Queen Victoria dominated the King's Walk and there were august pillars at the entrance to each college, immaculate lawns and sparkling lakes. When I arrived, a game of polo was going on, a band was playing on the green and razor-sharp cadets were practising sword drills. I was entranced by the place's air of endeavour and affluence.

Along with the rest of the Instructor Cadre 1998 intake, I went to Victory College to meet our teachers. 'Most of you won't be here after the first five weeks of beasting,' said Regimental Sergeant Major Kevin Roberts, a giant Welsh Guard.

Atholl Stewart and I were the only Black Watch candidates and we knew the stakes were high. There were 72 people competing for just 26 places and no one from our regiment had ever failed. We had been groomed for this and risked abject humiliation if we didn't win a place. Success would mean immediate promotion to colour sergeant and later to sergeant major, with the prospect of becoming a commissioned officer.

Several other candidates had been at Shorncliffe at the same time as I had. This was proof of the excellence of the Infantry Junior Leaders' training. Sadly, the scheme was scrapped in the early '90s as part of a cost-cutting exercise.

Selection began as soon as we met our instructors in the bar on the first night. We had to wear lounge suits. Fortunately, I was a suit-and-tie man. The beer was free and some of the guys had a bit too much. I was careful, sensing that the instructors were observing our social skills. We were being watched all the time. What exactly were they looking for? 'It's difficult to define,' I was told. 'But if you have it, we will find it. And if you don't, you won't make it.'

It was probably the most intensive course I've ever been on, with a major physical test six days a week. In the first five weeks, we experienced what we might put cadets through in a year. We were up from dawn until late at night, preparing several lessons, of which we might give one the next day. Other candidates were your 'students' as you taught weapons training, map-reading drill and physical fitness, watched by several instructors. We had to develop a new teaching style, radically different from the aggressive approach usually taken with young recruits. Some of us would soon be training the elite: princes, the sons of presidents and generals of friendly countries and late-entry officer recruits such as doctors and lawyers in their 40s and 50s. Shouting at them wouldn't work. We had to think laterally and make our lessons stimulating.

The atmosphere was fiercely competitive. Only one in three of us would pass and failures were dismissed each week. Eleven of us came from Scottish regiments and we Jocks stuck together. If one of us gave a lesson, the rest were especially attentive, asking helpful questions and holding up prompts that the instructors at the back couldn't see. But if our 'teacher' was a nob, we showed no enthusiasm. The Jocks met nightly to discuss who had given a bad lesson and was likely to be sent home. We marked his name on a list and, after the sound of the highlighter pen, called him a 'zzuh'. 'He's a zzuh,' we'd mutter hopefully as an arsehole walked by. Sometimes, this sound would echo around the classroom but only we knew what it meant.

Each Saturday, you went before your platoon instructors, a colour sergeant and a major. I liked my colour sergeant, a paratrooper, but I thought the young major was a bit of a numpty. While non-commissioned officers sweated blood to win a place at the Academy, commissioned officers just needed a recommendation by a peer. I had more respect for the colour sergeants because they had earned the right to teach the army's future leaders.

We had to complete peer-assessment forms commenting on the performances of other candidates. This was meant to test our integrity but we called it 'slate a mate'. In the interview, they always criticised us about something. This was disconcerting if you were used to being a top soldier in your regiment. However, we discovered that we were all getting the same treatment and at least we weren't told to pack our bags.

Most Saturday nights, I went downtown with good pals like 'TB' – Tam Brass – and 'Cammy' – Alan Cameron – who always came back singing 'Mack the Knife'. I had to keep telling him to shut up or we'd be in trouble.

After three months, the last forty candidates were summoned to a room where a pile of brown envelopes lay on a table. 'Take yours and don't open it until you are back in your room,' said the colour sergeant. Of course, I opened mine straight away. Glimpsing 'congratulations', I sauntered, relieved, down the corridor.

In my best kit, I joined the parade before General Arthur Denaro, the commandant of the academy. He shook our hands and presented us with crowns to place above our three stripes. We were now colour sergeants.

TB and I proudly wore our new Sandhurst ties when we hired a car to drive back to Edinburgh. Happy but dangerously exhausted, we took turns ploughing up the motorway on a shivery night. We were on the A74, with me at the wheel and Tam asleep, when the Nissan Primera hit black ice and scraped along the inside-lane crash barrier. A back door was ripped off and the car started spinning. I feared the worst for my precious portable TV on the back seat. Tam woke up and assumed a crash position. 'Stand by for the flip!' I screamed. We rolled all the way over and landed upright, on three wheels, in the slow lane. 'Fuck me, that was close!'

There was a draught by my left ear. Then I saw that Tam's door was wide open and he was running up the road like Forrest Gump. I looked in my rear-view mirror. Horn blaring, an articulated lorry was bearing down on me. I've just passed that shit course and now I'm going to die, I thought. I sat, trapped by my seat belt, as the lorry swerved past, rattling the car with vibrations.

My TV was wrecked. The car was a write-off, too, but somehow we drove to a slip road and summoned a recovery vehicle.

Back at Sandhurst, I completed another three months' continuation training and was ranked as one of the few instructors allowed to teach in both of the Academy's colleges. I was appointed the colour-sergeant instructor of commissioning course CC982. These cadets had done three months' weapons training at Old College and I had to take them through their last nine months at New College. Their morale was low, which was unsurprising, as they were trailing along in last place in the prestigious annual Sovereign's Platoon competition. I got the impression that their previous instructor had been something of a bully.

In my number-one dress order – kilt, spats and blue bonnet – I started to instil a new confidence in my cadets. I went round the room asking everyone why they were here. There was a mix of military ambitions. When one guy said he wanted to join the SAS, everyone laughed. I later discovered that he was nicknamed 'Bullet' because people thought he was a bit slow. 'Stop laughing,' I barked. 'We are starting with a clean slate. We will prepare afresh for the Sovereign's Platoon competition and this is the last day that any of you will come last.'

My platoon included several foreign notables such as Mr Kobwe, son of a senior minister in Lesotho, and Mr Logvinenko, son of a former Russian general. Tam Brass's platoon included Mr Hamzah, the heir to the Jordanian throne. His younger brother Prince Hashim followed him to the academy while I was there and I taught them both. There was also an opulent sprinkling of Saudi princes. I was proud that the overseas cadets saw us as incorruptible (we had been taught to refuse offers of gifts without causing offence). However, the princes were allowed to join us for an end-of-year party, when they took us in stretch limos for a VIP night at Stringfellows.

Richie Forsyth was the lone Jock in my platoon, the son of the Black Watch padre and a terrific sportsman. I later heard that he was rejected for an officer's post by the Black Watch board at Sandhurst solely because of his Scottish accent. This was an example of how our regiment was in the grip of 'Surrey Highlanders' schooled at Eton and Harrow. Richie went off to join the King's Own Scottish Borderers instead.

I used humour to develop camaraderie. Peter 'Corky' Corcoran had been breaking the rules by entertaining 'Foxy', an attractive female officer cadet, in his room. Corky was a charming chap with a cut-glass accent. One morning, it was suggested to me that I should inspect his locker. Usually, I looked in the cadets' rooms but not in their lockers. I decided to have some fun.

'Good morning, Colour Sergeant, how are you this morning?' said Corky.

'Let's have a look in your locker,' I replied.

'I beg your pardon, Colour Sergeant?'

'Open your fucking locker!'

Sure enough, inside hung two green army-issue skirts. Corky was an enthusiastic ironer and had been giving Foxy a helping hand.

'Whose are these?' I asked.

'I'm sure I don't know, Colour Sergeant.'

'Well, they must be yours then.'

'Yes, Colour Sergeant.'

'Well, you'd better put one on and get yourself out on muster parade.'

Corky appeared on the square in his shirt and tie, boots and green skirt. He did an elegant right marker, advancing 14 paces in front of everyone, while Foxy covered her face, surrounded by giggling comrades.

Angus McAfee, my platoon commander, was a small, athletic guy with a wild sense of humour. At first, we didn't hit it off, probably because I sometimes came across as a rigid Black Watch diehard. But that soon changed. One day, he raised an unexpected problem.

'Colour,' he said, 'I think there's a lot of frustration among the men.'

'Why's that, sir?' I asked, expecting complaints about my rigorous training regime.

'Well, I don't think they're shagging.'

'What? What evidence do you have, sir?' I asked.

'Well, some of the girls are telling me that the boys are ignoring them.'

Our company was two platoons of thirty men and a platoon of young women living on the floor above them.

Angus explained his plan and we went into town to buy a selection of the loudest bow ties on offer. At muster parade the next morning, two buxom female cadets presented me with ceremonial cushions laid out with dicky bows. Then I addressed the male cadets. 'It has been brought to my attention by my intelligence sources that a number of you haven't had a good shag yet. Now, you can't command men in battle and face death if you haven't had a good shag. The girls have given me the names of some men they think are still virgins. It has been decided that, instead of ties, you will wear dicky bows at supper until it is independently corroborated that you can wear a tie again.' It was all tongue-in-cheek and seemed to work, because the girls stopped complaining that the men weren't paying them enough attention.

Morale soared as my platoon's performance improved. They learned to work together. In the indoor assault course, for example, they had to help slower team members over the obstacles. We started winning and moved steadily up the league table from tenth to first place. Against the odds, we became the Sandhurst champions.

We won privileges as that year's Sovereign's Platoon and were invited to Buckingham Palace to troop the new Sandhurst colours, presented every 25 years, in front of Her Majesty. Sharon and I and the rest of the command group went to meet the Queen upstairs in the Yellow Drawing Room.

'You're pregnant,' she said to Sharon, who was seven months gone.

'We have a difficulty, Your Majesty,' I said. 'I'm Scottish, Sharon is from Ireland and our baby will be born in England.'

'Ah, well, at least the baby will be British,' replied the Queen.

I spoke about the time in the late '80s when the Black Watch had guarded Balmoral. I was in a Land Rover driven by a Jock called 'Monster' when the young Prince William flagged us down. He was in a hurry to get back to the castle.

'Go faster, go faster!' he ordered Monster.

'I cannae go any faster in these grounds.'

'Go faster or I'll tell my daddy!'

'Shut up, you wee fucker!'

Monster slammed on the brakes and made the second in line to the throne get out and walk.

The Queen laughed at my edited version of this story. 'William could be horrid at times but he's better now,' she said.

At Sandhurst, it was the norm to mix with royalty and celebrities. I had a good chat at the bar with Prince Charles once about his family's close connection to the Black Watch. His grandmother, the Queen Mother, was colonel-in-chief and her brother died fighting with the regiment in the First World War.

Henry Cooper floored me when he visited for a boxing tournament. He wanted to get off early, so I called him a lightweight and asked him out for a fight. 'All right,' he said. 'You Jocks are well known for your heavyweight champions.'

By contrast, Jim Davidson struck me as an insecure wee man who liked to wear tartan trousers to remind everyone that his dad was a Jock. In the bar one night, he passed round a handwritten note meant to reach a female staff sergeant. When it got to me, I opened it and deciphered the scrawled message, which said something like, 'Would you like to be wife number four?' With a smile, I waved the note at him and screwed it up.

After our victory in the Sovereign's Platoon, I was appointed the general's stick orderly colour sergeant, responsible for assisting the Sandhurst commandant with his many ceremonial duties. This proved tricky one Sunday morning when, with a thousand men waiting outside the C. of E. church, the general woke with a hangover and decided to attend the Catholic chapel instead. Another time, as we were rehearsing the Sovereign's Parade, the general strolled up with his three dogs. 'Can't be bothered taking the salute this morning, Colour. Get yourself up there.' I happily climbed onto the dais and played general for a couple of hours.

Our success in the competition meant that I was the first Black Watch soldier listed on the board of honour in the academy library. I'm hugely proud that many of my cadets went on to build strong careers – and that includes 'Bullet', who fulfilled his ambition and is now an SAS troop commander.

After the Sovereign's Parade, we were each allowed one guest at a party in the Indian Army Memorial Library. I brought my mum to her first military function since my passing-out parade at Shorncliffe in 1984. It was her birthday. At the formal lunch, I got the band to play 'Happy Birthday' for her and all my cadets stood up to sing. The academy sergeant major approached me, saying, 'The general would like to speak to you outside with your guest.' Mum and I went out to meet two generals – the Sandhurst commandant and his friend, a guest of honour from the SAS.

'You must be very proud of him,' said one of them to Mum.

'Oh, yes!' she replied, reaching up to squeeze my cheek.

Somewhere, there is a photo of me, bright red, looking at her while the generals laugh.

Not long after that came an even prouder day. In the early hours of 24 May 1999, I rushed Sharon to hospital and she gave birth to our beautiful daughter Hannah. I burst into tears as I held our baby in my arms for the first time. It was a moment that will stay with me for ever.

• • •

My next challenge was to train two teams to compete in the Sandhurst Cup at the United States Military Academy at West Point. I arranged a three-stage selection and chose twenty-two team

members, including four women, from the ninety applicants. Then
I flew to New York to visit West Point and learn more about the
tough one-day military-skills competition.

It was February 2000 and so cold that you could have skated on
the Hudson River, which ran alongside the academy. In 1778, during
America's Revolutionary War with Britain, George Washington saw
West Point's strategic importance and built a fortress there. After
independence, it became the United States Military Academy. It was
a grand institution, where 4,000 cadets dined together in a giant hall
with endless tables. It was like a scene from Hogwarts.

When I came back with my teams in April, the sun was shining
and our opponents were feisty. We marched past a sea of banners
hanging from every window, declaring 'Beat the Brits' or 'Down
with the Brits'. As the only British competitors, we faced scores
of American teams and two from Canada. However, we were
thoroughly prepared for the gruelling nine-mile course, which was
punctuated with a variety of challenges such as marksmanship, rope-
bridge building and rowing. Everything was done using American
equipment and to American standards. The climax was a two-mile
run, carrying rigid inflatable boats above shoulder height. I ran round
with both my teams and was quietly ecstatic when the final results
were announced in front of a crowd of thousands.

We had won first and third place. The Canadians came second
but that didn't stop the Yanks jumping and hollering whenever an
American went on stage to collect an individual trophy. 'Don't be
making arseholes of yourselves,' I told my teams when it was our
turn. We marched up like true Brits, crisply and silently, to collect
the prized Sandhurst Sword.

Despite the competitiveness, the Yanks treated us with hospitality.
I had a memorable meeting with the West Point commander. 'Come
in and have a chat, Colour,' he drawled, ushering me into his office,
where he was sprawled on a chesterfield suite, chomping on a huge
cigar and guarded by two pistol-toting cut-outs of John Wayne.

• • •

Professionally, I'd had two hugely successful years (despite a traumatic turn when I almost died of septicaemia) but a growing personal crisis tainted these triumphs. Sharon and I were living increasingly separate lives. She was a midwife and focused on her career, while I was thoroughly immersed in mine. I am sure we both meant our marriage to be 'until death do us part' but life got in the way. When the Black Watch was posted to Fallingbostel, Germany, in November 2000, Sharon returned to Belfast for good, taking 18-month-old Hannah with her. Desolate, I threw myself deeper into work.

The Black Watch was converting into an armoured infantry regiment. We were given a fleet of 50 armoured Warrior Infantry Fighting Vehicles and I began intense training as a gunner. Frank Mason, a talented guy from the Royal Highland Fusiliers, was brought in to manage the training. I relished this new challenge and got top grades. At first, the Warrior seemed impressive, a sturdy and speedy beast, but we were soon disillusioned with its chain-gun weapon system. Our instructors spent an alarming amount of time teaching us stoppage drills and we had countless stoppages on the firing range, when everyone had to sit in their turrets for ten minutes, waiting for the jammed gun to 'cool off'. If we didn't let it cool down, Frank explained, the ammunition might explode in our faces.

The instructors gave us the low-down on the gun's history. The gist of it was that it had been bought 'off the shelf' from the Americans and we just had to get on with it. An improved version of the Warrior – the Desert Warrior, with a new turret and the more reliable Bushmaster chain gun – was being exported to Kuwait but it was not available to British troops.

I was happy to be back in Charlie Company – working with our commander, Ed Jones, and sergeant major, Harry Lawrence – as we prepared for an imminent posting to Kosovo. At a social event one Saturday night, Harry kindly listened to my marriage woes. Grateful for his sympathy, I wished Harry and his wife Donna goodnight.

The next morning, Jimmy Russell called me with shocking news. 'Donna is dead,' he said. 'Harry woke up and found her dead beside him. It was a brain haemorrhage.' Poor Harry was devastated. The job was irrelevant now. What did he care about Kosovo when he had two motherless children to care for? Mike Riddell-Webster, who had risen to become commanding officer of the Black Watch, asked me to take on Harry's role. It was painful to accept the job in those circumstances. I felt Harry's deep sorrow as we embraced before he went on extended leave. He is a great father.

As company sergeant major, I was paired with Ed Jones in the command vehicle, Zero Bravo. I looked my new Warrior up and down and noticed a word stencilled on the side of the turret.

'Why is this called Christine?' I asked Willie Anderson, our driver.

'Because she's just like a woman: temperamental and liable to break down when you least expect it.'

I got my first taste of Christine's moods when we took her to Poland on Exercise Ulan Eagle, a combat training exercise. As we drove through a ravine, one of her tracks snapped and a CRARRV – the British Army's largest land vehicle – had to drag her out, leaving behind a trail of crushed trees. What if this happens on a battlefield? I wondered.

• • •

On a sunny May day in 2001, we flew into Pristina, the Kosovan capital, a city surrounded by hills and racked by conflict. First, the Serbs had suppressed the Albanians, driving them from their homes. Then NATO intervened against the Serbs and the Albanian Kosovo Liberation Army turned the tables on them. Many Serbs had fled Pristina and the houses of those left were often surrounded by protective barbed wire. Our main job was to patrol the streets, keeping the peace while ready for war. Charlie Company was based in Portakabins in a police compound infested with vermin. Our beat included the long Dardania Tunnel. It hid human and animal corpses and stank of death.

In August, some of our men were assigned to fly to Macedonia with a fleet of armoured vehicles to support the SAS. They were joining Taskforce Harvest, a mission to bolster the neighbouring Macedonian government by disarming ethnic Albanian insurgents. It was a NATO operation and no one told the Russians, who weren't members of NATO but had troops in Kosovo as part of KFOR, the international peacekeeping force in the territory. There had already been a showdown between British and Russian troops at Pristina airport in 1999 and when we turned up there with a big armoured convoy Russian soldiers refused to open the barrier. I pushed it up by hand and we filed past them, making our way to a giant Galaxy plane. The Russians then lined up in force and it took a series of phone calls to defuse the tension. The Jocks flew to Macedonia and two weeks later they all came back safely.

On 11 September, I was in a bar in Tirana, the capital of Albania, when the TV showed chilling images of the two planes smashing into the twin towers of the World Trade Center in New York. I had been to the city during my trip to West Point. Like millions around the world, I was transfixed as these landmarks collapsed, killing thousands. I sensed that this meant war.

• • •

Rab Donkin was a strong, affable young Jock. He had been out of action with an injury and I was happy to oblige when he asked to join us in Kosovo. He became my driver and also took part in Taskforce Harvest. At the end of the tour, in November 2001, he volunteered to help guard our vehicles when they were taken by train to the Greek port of Thessaloniki.

The train reached a place in Macedonia where Albanian insurgents had lowered electricity pylons to ambush us. As he sat on top of a 432 AFV armoured personnel carrier, Rab received a massive electric shock from a live cable. Corporal Colin Hamilton rushed to his aid and was also shocked. He lost a leg. Rab never regained consciousness. His condition steadily deteriorated and he died in hospital in Birmingham.

I felt responsible. Never before had I lost a man on an operation. As company sergeant major, I met Rab's family in Rosyth and they vented their grief and anger. 'The arrangements must be exactly as you want them,' I said. Then I met the vicar to discuss the service and trained the funeral party that carried Rab's coffin. It was draped in a Union Jack and I was choking with grief as I handed it to Rab's parents at his graveside.

SEVEN

Taking on Saddam

On our return from the Balkans, Charlie Company embarked on a 12-month combat-training programme. Fortuitously, this coincided with the long build-up to the invasion of Iraq. British forces were already engaged with the Americans in Afghanistan and it was clear that George Bush had his sights set on Saddam Hussein. When we sat in Warrior simulators in Sennelager, there were maps of Iraq on our screens. War seemed inevitable and I was determined that my men would be trained and prepared. As sergeant major of a specialist weapons company, I was becoming increasingly aware of equipment failings. It was particularly unsettling knowing that my Warrior was a flawed beast and that I could not rely upon the chain gun.

I was still feeling pain from my break-up with Sharon and guilt that I couldn't always be there for Hannah, watching her grow. I was weary of my single life and intrigued when Frank Mason invited me to a formal dinner, telling me, 'There's someone I want you to meet.'

Rachel and I sat together at the table chatting about our different experiences of military life. I'd never socialised with anyone from the military police and her previous dealings with the Black Watch had been strictly professional. 'We're usually locking you lot up on a Saturday night,' she joked. We arranged to meet again and our relationship blossomed.

In July 2002, the Black Watch Battle Group flew to Calgary and travelled on to Medicine Hat, heading for a six-week exercise at BATUS (the British Army Training Unit Suffield). Set in the Canadian prairies, it covers an area the size of Wales and is the British army's biggest training zone. Because it is extremely isolated, soldiers can practise warfare on a relatively large scale without causing danger or disturbance to civilians.

We were soon involved in realistic mock combat – the infantry fanning out in battle formation supported by Warriors, tanks and helicopters – but without the blood and stress. Our weapons were fitted with lasers and the TESEX (tactical effects simulation exercise) system monitored hits and kills. Hits automatically disabled engines and umpires kept a sharp eye out for cheating. Our opponents, the 9th/12th Royal Lancers, readily exploited our weaknesses. One afternoon, as we took orders from the commanding officer with our vehicles reversed into a tight protective circle, the enemy swept back and forth through the valley in a triumphant ambush. Vehicles and men bleeped away as we suffered heavy 'losses'.

We were allocated Warriors when we got to BATUS and I had been happy to leave Christine behind. However, I learned that problems were rife with the vehicle when mine broke down on an exercise. We took it to the 'sin bin' and found another 15 Warriors being repaired there.

Our crew included the company commander, Ed Jones, and driver Willie Anderson. One sunny afternoon, Ed was quietly preparing for a 5 p.m. orders meeting with the CO, sitting in the back of the Warrior with the rear door open and his legs over the side. I told Willie to switch the engine on so that we could boil up some water in the bercol (the kettle below the driver's seat) and make a brew. Suddenly, I heard a metallic whir and then a yell from Ed. I looked back to see him caught in the rear door, which was trying to close itself. I scrambled to the back of the vehicle and Ed wrapped his arms around me, screaming in agony as four brutal tons of metal crushed him. It was the cry of a man who knows that his legs are about to be sliced off at the knees.

'Switch the engine off!' I bawled to Willie. Thank God, Willie cut the power before the door finally slammed shut. I laid Ed down in the back of the Warrior and examined his legs. They were slashed and bleeding, with clear indentations on both kneecaps. Fortunately, there appeared to be no broken bones.

'My mother would not have appreciated my screaming like that,' said Ed.

Both Ed's parents had died that year in quick succession and, as a single guy with no family in Britain, he'd coped with the loss alone.

'Your mother wouldn't have appreciated meeting you so soon,' I replied, as he pulled up his trousers, grabbed his notebook and limped off to his meeting.

It was typical of Ed not to make a fuss. A tall, unworldly, gangly man, 'Mr Bean' was very well liked. The Jocks sometimes called the pair of us 'Jeeves and Wooster'. Ed took a genuine interest in the welfare of his troops and spent time asking them about their families and careers. He was passionate about training and development, and he encouraged promotions.

His leadership style was drastically different to that of many of the officers, who lacked empathy with the Jocks. They would threaten people with poor reports to get results and could be ruthless – not as warriors but in a selfish, spiteful way. Several times, I heard these contemptuous words: 'You should have gone to university and then you might be an officer.' The Jocks from Charlie Company were skilled weapons specialists in their late 20s and 30s and they didn't like it when young officers, fresh from college, talked to them as if they were 17 year olds. It wasn't just a matter of age: they wanted to be treated with respect. Ed understood this.

Back in Germany, Rachel had a tempting suggestion for me: 'What do you think about getting a flat together?' We had missed each other and the thought of escaping from the single men's quarters in Fallingbostel was very appealing. We went flat hunting and soon set up home together in Hohne.

My life was improving just as the war clouds gathered. In

September 2002, President Bush addressed the UN, calling for action against Iraq, and Tony Blair published his famous dossier claiming that Saddam had an arsenal of chemical, biological and nuclear weapons and that some of these weapons of mass destruction could be deployed within 45 minutes of his giving the order to use them. Saddam let UN weapons inspectors into Iraq but it still seemed likely that we would have to go and secure his WMDs.

News spread unofficially that the Black Watch Battle Group (two armoured infantry companies each made up of about 150 men and 15 Warriors, supported by engineers, artillery and armoured-vehicle platoons) would be in the front line as part of the 7th Armoured Brigade, the Desert Rats. Brigades are usually triangular, with three regiments. Ours had been strengthened to a square, with two infantry and two armoured regiments. The Black Watch would be joined by the Royal Regiment of Fusiliers, the Royal Tank Regiment and the Royal Scots Dragoon Guards.

Ed had finished his two-year appointment as company commander and James Ord, back from the SAS, replaced him. I'd known and liked James for more than a decade. He was a man of fewer words than Ed, so I might have to take on more of the pastoral side of the job than before, but I trusted him and knew that he had plenty of grit: a good man to go to war with.

Just after Christmas, Riddell-Webster made a rare address to the regiment. All leave was cancelled and all posts were frozen, he announced. We must prepare to go to Kuwait. We immediately set about repainting our vehicles, including the Warriors, replacing the standard camouflage with a light-brown desert hue. 'Look, sir, this paint is shite!' said one man, reviewing the results of his efforts. Sure enough, it had started to flake off in the fluttering German snow. It was water-based paint – perhaps not the smartest choice. We crossed our fingers as we dispatched all the heavy armour to Kuwait by sea.

MI6 officers came and gave us briefings about the evils of the enemy. They showed us maps of Iraq pocked with alleged missile sites. We were going to Basra, they said, where we'd find plenty of

WMDs. Video footage showed the gassing of thousands of Kurds, highlighting the barbarity of the regime. Speakers focused on the abuse of women. Saddam's sons trawled the streets at night, looking for fresh victims to rape and murder. In Kuwait in 1990, Iraqi soldiers returned over a period of weeks to take turns raping a man's four daughters, until the men got bored and killed the whole family. By the end of the presentations, we were all firmly of the belief that we were going to clear out the Devil himself.

Our training was stepped up. When two of my Jocks fell asleep in a medical presentation given by James, I dragged them down to the front of the lecture theatre. 'If you get involved in a firefight with these guys, be very scared,' I fumed. 'The fuckers can't keep their eyes open.' It was harsh but I wanted everyone to appreciate the seriousness of the challenge ahead. Tragically, one of the men I singled out that day was killed in an accident on the road to Camp Dogwood in October 2004.

In February, we began taking a medley of drugs, including the nightmare-inducing malaria tablets. The invasion seemed inevitable, even though it lacked UN backing and more than a million people marched against it in London. Although I wasn't convinced about the WMDs, I still believed that it was right to end Saddam's tyranny. It annoyed me, though, when my experienced Warrior crew was replaced on the eve of war. I had to train my new driver, Lee Kirby, from scratch. Rachel flew to Kuwait with the Royal Military Police at the end of the month, a week before me. We spent an emotional few days together before she departed for the unknown.

Terminal D at Hanover airport is reserved for military flights and on 3 March I sat there with most of Charlie Company, chatting to Colonel Kevin Beaton, the battle group's senior medical officer, who would later become my boss. We expected to board a Hercules and were surprised to discover that we were flying on a Boeing 747 with an Icelandic civilian crew. Everything seemed rushed.

At Kuwait airport, a blast of heat greeted us and American troops, who were clearly running the show, directed us to mandatory briefings on NBC warfare. We were driven out into the desert and issued with white cards listing more robust rules of engagement than the yellow ones that had guided us in Northern Ireland. I noted that we no longer had to shout a warning before shooting at someone who was shooting at us.

The Black Watch Battle Group was based at Camp Coyote. We slept on the floors of Bedouin tents, each holding 100 men. In my light sleeping bag, the March nights were freezing. Sandstorms were so severe that, if you didn't count the paces, you could get lost coming back from the cookhouse. On our arrival in Kuwait, a BBC camera crew wanted to embed itself with my commander but he was having none of it. 'Please get rid,' he said to me. 'Offload them onto the anti-tank platoon.' Meanwhile, the Jocks were pissed off when I was ordered to lock up their mobiles – many of them had bought dual-band phones for texting home from Kuwait. I allowed each platoon a turn on my satellite phone so that people could call their families.

We readied ourselves and – because of the shortage of decent equipment – improvised. We had CamelBaks (special water-carrying rucksacks) to drink from on the battlefield only because Captain Paddy Nichol, a multimillionaire who had served with the regiment, had bought them for us. On my recommendation, the men from Charlie Company each spent £250 from their wages on combat assault vests. Unlike the army-issue webbing, these vests had pouches at the front so that you could keep water, pistols and other essentials to hand. Many of us did not have desert boots and Major Lindsay MacDuff was going around with body armour crudely taped to his uniform. We weren't happy to learn that the Americans had christened British troops in Kuwait 'the Borrowers'. They banned us from entering their camps except on official business, fearing that our evident lack of equipment might affect morale.

Then our Warriors were delivered to the camp. They were a sorry-looking sight. Much of the paint had come off, leaving a scruffy mixture of colours. The Jocks, watching with wry smiles, whistled the *Steptoe and Son* theme tune as their vehicles came off low-loaders looking like they'd already been to war.

We took NAPS tablets to counteract nerve gas and carried our respirators everywhere, ready for the frequent Scud alarms. Occasionally, these were justified and we would hear the thud of missiles hitting the sand beyond our camp. The alarm sounded one day as we sat in the briefing tent within a crucible of defensively parked vehicles. Saddam could have set his watch by Mike Riddell-Webster's orders meetings – he always held them at 5 p.m. As the siren blared, a dozen of us dived under the table – not that this would offer much protection. Then we heard Colour Sergeant Rab Penman shouting, 'You've nicked my mask, you bastard!' Rab had dragged Mike Williamson out from under the table and was trying to pull the respirator off his head! Unlike Mike, Rab always kept his kit together. James and I shuddered with laughter behind our masks. It was like a scene from *Carry On Scud*. Eventually, Rab gave up and jumped into the back of a Warrior, slamming the door behind him.

Charlie Company was in the forward position in the camp, facing the enemy. Our usual Scud routine was to mask up, jump into our vehicles and sit, sometimes for hours, sipping water through straws and waiting for the all-clear. I often grabbed a kip while some of the Jocks, I later learned, stopped bothering with the masks and had a good chinwag instead.

Preparations accelerated and we began nightly exercises in which we lined up in formation and practised crossing the border, 30 km ahead. We made a 200-km round trip to an American camp for firing practice. It was a memorable journey because, caught in a sandstorm, we came dangerously close to some US artillery and nearly got zapped in a 'blue on blue', or 'friendly fire', blunder. But we made it to the camp and were dazzled by the sight of enough attack helicopters to fill several football pitches. As usual, we Brits were badly equipped. I had a pathetic fifty rounds for the chain gun and three for the Rarden cannon.

When we'd been in Kuwait for a week or two, Dr Lewis Moonie MP, a junior defence minister, came to see us. I remembered the time when he had visited us before at Fallingbostel. The officers had made a fuss of him but I'd tried a different tack. 'Can you please fix the traffic lights outside the Queen Margaret's Hospital in Dumfermline?' I'd said. 'They're a nightmare.' Moonie had laughed and he made a beeline for me now at Camp Coyote. We slipped away from his minders and he rolled a cigarette. 'I'm really sorry that this is happening,' he said. 'Let me know if there's anything you need.' I told him about the problems with our uniform but went easy on him. I liked the man and thought he was genuine.

When US officers from the 1st Marine Expeditionary Force (1MEF) came to our camp to make a presentation, the Jocks' consensus was 'what a bunch of tossers'. The gung-ho fighter pilots provided good movie-style entertainment, chomping on cigars, boasting about their gear and promising the Iraqis 'death from above, fire from below'. They'd torch the place and then we'd sweep it up – that was the essence of their story. But the reality in southern Iraq would be very different.

It took me a while to locate Rachel but at last we caught up and we stood together as US Commander Tommy Franks addressed the 7th Armoured Brigade, preparing us for imminent war. It was a powerful speech, theatrically punctuated by overflying jets and ending with: 'We'll bomb the bastards!'

On 19 March, as the first US bunker busters and cruise missiles hit Baghdad, we reached our designated concentration point close to the border wall, code-named 'Barnsley'. In the fading light, I scanned our sea of armour and waved to my good friend Stevie Anderson, sergeant major of Delta Company. Will we both make it? I wondered.

We had nothing to do but grab some sleep and wait for the order to advance. 'Put the engine on and we'll brew up,' I shouted to Lee.

Silence.

'Get a move on – we're parched!'

'I think it's knackered, sir.'

Christine – the company commander's vehicle – had thrown another hissy fit as we stood on the brink of war. We called for a REME (Royal Electrical and Mechanical Engineers) crew to come and fix her. Sergeant Tim Curtis and Corporal Carl Frost had a look and announced that we'd have to do a full engine-pack lift. This was heavy work and we all mucked in. Soon, Christine's guts were lying all over the sand and the REME crew were painstakingly searching for the fault. Minutes and then hours passed. 'It's got to be ready by four,' James told me. 'If not, we'll have to leave her here and commandeer another vehicle.'

At last, Tim had 'good' news. 'This cable has melted in the heat,' he told me. 'We'll have to do a botch job for now.' We replaced the engine pack and they soldered the cable, patching it with insulating tape. Then the engine coughed and we helped the REME crew quickly pack up their gear and get out of the way.

At 0445 hours, helicopters flew over us, followed by the flashes of rockets speeding into Iraq. We were locked down in the turret of the Warrior waiting for the word to come through on the radio.

'Breach done!'

The Royal Regiment of Fusiliers had blown five holes in the border wall to confuse the enemy. We needed only one and slowly we advanced to it, following a rehearsed order of march. Cylumes (light sticks) and torches lit up our path. The military police controlled the flow of traffic and I wondered how Rachel was. When would we meet again? The wall was about 20 ft high; it reminded me of Berlin. Our engineers had cleared mines and placed a small bridge over the rubble of the breach wall to smooth our path. 'Welcome to Iraq,' said a sign they had prepared earlier. 'Bridge crossing sponsored by 1RRF Battle Group.'

My adrenalin pumped, counteracting my sleeplessness, as we passed the burning wreckages of an old Soviet troop carrier and a T-54 tank. Advancing at a brisk 25 kph, I kept traversing the turret 360 degrees but there was no enemy in sight. We cut across the Route 6 highway, passing a sign, in Arabic and English, for Baghdad. It was bullet-pocked and hanging loose, like something from a dusty Wild West scene in a film. As the sky brightened, it dawned on me that normal rules didn't apply any more. It was dog eat dog.

EIGHT

One Man Down

We pressed on through the desert, eyes alert for enemy activity and ears wired to the radio. Black Watch armoured vehicles stretched for miles from the border as we headed towards Az Zubayr. I had never before been part of an invading force. When would the enemy attack us? Would we hit booby traps or mines? But nothing stopped us. Occasionally, we passed sandbagged military posts but they were abandoned. At dusk, we dimly spied our first locals, scurrying from an entrance to the oil refinery with what looked like computers, furniture and boxes before disappearing into the gloom.

At about 2000 hours, we reached the concentration point set up by the American 1MEF, a few miles south of Az Zubayr and well protected by their Abrams tanks. Our CO had met their commanders and James came back from a briefing with a big change of plan. 'The Americans are leaving and pushing north,' he said. 'We're in charge now. The 7th Armoured Brigade is no longer a relief-in-place force. We're a tactical-assault force tasked with taking control of Az Zubayr and then liberating Basra.' My heart quickened. This meant undiluted war. I had spent years training for this moment in my career. It was a challenge most people would never face.

We had already been briefed about Az Zubayr. This strategic town was our gateway to the main prize of Basra, Iraq's second-biggest city. Az Zubayr could prove tricky for us because most of its 300,000 inhabitants were Sunni Muslims like Saddam. They were more likely to back his regime than Basra's majority Shia Muslim population, as Saddam had savagely repressed followers of this branch of Islam. In Az Zubayr, we were to expect resistance from Saddam's loyal Fedayeen militia. There was a lot to think about but I was exhausted by the previous night's vigil and dozed off in the Warrior. It was the first of many nights that James and I spent cooped up together inside Christine's turret.

On the next day, 21 March, the pace quickened. The Americans were preparing to go to Baghdad. Atholl Stewart, sergeant major of Bravo Company, had set up a POW camp to take their prisoners. James briefed me. 'A party of marines has been ambushed,' he said. 'Several have been killed, including a woman. The Americans say they've caught the culprits and your job is to go and bring those prisoners back here.'

We set off, a four-ton cargo truck topped and tailed by two Warriors, using maps and satellite navigation to guide us to the village with the prisoners, which was about five kilometres away. It was a memorable journey, past roadside wells that spewed flaming oil. Thick black smoke obscured the dimming sun. In places, the earth was thick with seeping black gold. The enemy is close, I thought, setting fire to the wells and killing our allies.

The village was a little collection of shacks and some unfinished concrete buildings, one of them taken over by US marines. I went to see their surprisingly youthful commanding officer, who spoke in staccato sentences, as if in shock. 'They came from nowhere. RPGed a Humvee. There was no sign of them. Then, bam! Two of our guys are dead. We pursued them. Surrounded the village. They surrendered.'

He took me to the prisoners, who were in two rooms: sixteen Iraqi soldiers lying on the floor in one and four officers smoking in another. As I looked down at the officers, one stood up and came towards me, smiling.

'I am officer,' he said.

'You're a prisoner,' I replied and turned to walk out of the room.

I felt a flutter of incredulous anger. This guy was pretending to be my mate when he had just killed some of our friends! And he was angling for special treatment as an officer. That's the wrong move, sunshine, I thought.

'Thank you, we'll take charge of them now,' I said to the American commander, before going to speak to my men. I instructed them to form a line down the corridor and out of the building and to take turns grabbing a prisoner and making him run out to the lorry, where two Jocks were waiting to lift him up and sit him down facing into the canvas cover. 'Make sure they keep their hands on their heads at all times,' I said. 'No need to be brutal but they need to know who's in charge and that if they try anything we'll shoot them.'

Fifteen minutes later, our twenty prisoners had no illusions about their status. We drove them back and delivered them one by one to Atholl Stewart's POW 'cage', which was in fact an area inside an abandoned warehouse that had been ringed with concertina barbed wire. All the prisoners were handcuffed and hooded with sandbags. We made them sit waiting for our intelligence teams, including Kuwaiti interpreters, who would interrogate them.

Over the 21st and 22nd, the 7th Armoured Brigade began surrounding Az Zubayr, taking control of all the arterial routes except the road into Basra. Several of us were blooded in the ensuing angry skirmishes and battles.

Corporal John Rose and his team from the mortar platoon got into a firefight when they drove past a big mosque on the edge of the town. Several weeks later, I wrote down his story when James and I were gathering evidence to make recommendations for bravery awards. 'We came under fire from the mosque,' he told me. 'First it was rifle fire and then an RPG went flying past. I decided to return the favour and so we dismounted and counter-attacked.' I chuckled at the thought. This was the mortar platoon, not infantrymen geared up for hand-to-hand fighting. A lot of them were a bit tubby.

More seriously, they had limited ammunition and soon ran out. 'A couple of us ran up to the window they'd been firing from and chucked in those new grenades we were given at Camp Coyote. Off they went and then all eight of us charged into the mosque, hoping to clear the bodies. But it turned out that those grenades were shite. The L2s would have done the business but instead we came into a room with six guys alive and shooting at us. So we retreated and lobbed in a couple more grenades. This time, we heard some groans and we stormed back in.'

Corporal Rose had wrestled the Iraqi commander to the ground and shot him dead with his own pistol. We sent off our report and Corporal Rose and Lance Corporal Laing were awarded the Military Cross for their actions in the operation.

On the 22nd, while John was attacking the militiamen in the mosque, Zero Bravo was taking part in the furious battle at the barracks. For hours, we confronted the enemy while grappling with chain-gun stoppages and the unspoken terror that Christine might conk out, leaving a bleak choice: stay sitting ducks or get out and fight our last fight. Somehow, we survived. The Delta Company team turned up with explosives and they ran with James back into the barracks to destroy the huge stocks of small arms, anti-tank weapons and RPGs. I kept guard, raining chain-gun fire on the advancing enemy and obliterating their technicals – the pick-up trucks with mounted machine guns – with the Rarden canon.

When we got back to relative safety, I felt the adrenalin ebbing quickly away. My combats had turned white from extreme perspiration and my hands were bloody and stinging with cuts and burns. Christine's front was thick with the refuse of combat – a mixture of thousands of empty 7.62-mm shells and hundreds of 30-mm ones from the Rarden cannon. I found a big brush to sweep them off.

'That was some fight, sir,' said Lee, my driver. 'I counted that you'd killed twenty of them before we pulled back to the barracks.'

Twenty dead. Was the total thirty? Or fifty? It was impossible to comprehend. Automatically, I mouthed a prayer for the departed and their loved ones. I recalled the guy in a red bandana who had kept jumping about firing at us. It had taken me a couple of chain-gun blasts to catch him and he'd cartwheeled in the air before crumpling into the dust.

Why? Why waste your life for Saddam? I tried to see it from their perspective. We were the invaders. What would I do if my country were occupied? Perhaps they had been told that we were coming to rape their women.

One thing I knew for sure: the Iraqis might have had a reputation for running away but I had seen no cowards that day.

• • •

The next morning, James and I discussed the previous day's work. We agreed that it was a job well done. If we had let the Iraqis recover their munitions, our men would have paid the price. And we had seen off some of their hardcore fighters. We were at war.

We went to assist with sniper ops. During the night, Sergeant Major 'Stew' Steward of the sniper platoon had dispatched his men to camouflaged positions in sheds, trees and dugout holes in the wasteland fringing the town. Their job was to flush out and kill Iraqi gunmen. Ours was to help them by using our times-eight sights and providing armoured back-up if needed.

Later that day, the 23rd, I heard that two Royal Engineers, Sapper Luke Allsopp and Staff Sergeant Simon Cullingworth, had been kidnapped in an ambush near Az Zubayr. It was very grim news.

Monday, 24 March was another eventful day. Back on sniper-support duties in the morning, we heard a distant clatter of machine-gun fire behind us. Later, I was surprised to see the CO of the Royal Tank Regiment get out of his vehicle. He had come to see James, who was his next-door neighbour in Germany. As I stood in the turret, I overheard them talking in an empty barn nearby.

'I've just lost one of my men,' said the CO. 'It was a blue on blue.'

'God, that's dreadful. The machine-gun fire earlier?' asked James.

'Yes. They were manning a vehicle checkpoint. There was a riot and the gunner on the Challenger opened up on a madman who was throwing rocks at Sergeant Roberts but he killed both of them.'

At the inquest in 2006, pathologists found that if Sergeant Steven Roberts had been wearing enhanced combat body armour – which should have been issued to troops before the war started – he would have survived.

In the afternoon, we moved to a new concentration point, 'the Crown Jewels', two miles north of Az Zubayr. Lee drove us through the sentry point and left past the CO's tent to park beside a tank ditch. We disembarked and enjoyed our dinner: boil-in-the-bag stew, chocolate, sweets and cups of tea. It was great to relax, behind a protective perimeter of tanks and lookouts, as the sun's heat waned. James was called to an orders meeting with the CO. Then the company radio crackled.

'Hello, Zero. This is 24 Alpha. Contact. Ambush. Wait. Out.'

Ambush! It was like an electric shock.

'Mount up!' I shouted to the crew, and we jumped back into the Warrior.

Tim Petransky sat in the back, peering at maps and maintaining radio contact with 24 Alpha. It was a Scimitar, part of a small convoy, with another Scimitar and a 432 personnel carrier, sent to reinforce beleaguered men from D Company at Bridge 4, a position at the Shatt al-Arab river. But the ambush was at the mosque. What on earth were they doing there? We had been told to stay well clear of it after John Rose's showdown on the 22nd, as it was taboo to storm a Muslim place of worship, even when the enemy used it as sanctuary to shoot at us. Our convoy must have taken a wrong turning and run into some raging hornets.

24 Alpha came on the radio again. 'Contact. We have bugged out. One man left behind.'

James came back and I quickly briefed him.

'Let's go now,' he said.

One of Charlie Company's men was missing. I visualised him surrounded by a howling mob. There had been no more news on the kidnapped Royal Engineers. We had to go immediately to bring our boy back. We raced south towards Az Zubayr.

Tim was hassling 24 Alpha on the radio. 'Send report of one man down,' he kept saying.

'Wait. Out,' was the repeated reply.

Then we got a report from the other Scimitar: 'Hello, Zero, this is 24. Contact with RPG and small arms. One man left behind and we have lost contact with the 432.'

They gave us the Zap (personal identification) number of the missing man and we worked out that he was Lance Corporal Barry Stephen. Then news came that the 432 had been located again. They had lost Barry after he bravely climbed onto their roof to fire at the enemy. At first, the others in the 432 didn't realise it but Barry must have been swept off the vehicle by an RPG that had been targeted just above them. We agreed to rendezvous at VCP2, a checkpoint manned by the Royal Engineers and military police at a junction where several roads merged into a single drag into town.

One of the two Scimitars had taken a turret strike and was out of action. Corporal Leathley commanded the other. I called him over.

'Do you know where Barry is?'

'I think so,' he answered. 'We came under fire from a shack in front of the mosque.'

'OK. Get back in your vehicle and let's go there.'

He paused, still in battle shock, and I needed to urge him on and back into action: 'Get in your fucking vehicle and let's go!'

'Yes, sir,' he replied, without further hesitation.

We were driving and firing: one vehicle laid down covering fire as another advanced and then we swapped roles. It was a pitch-dark night, with no ambient light except the flicker of oil wells burning in the distance. We could just make out the outline of the mosque. In daylight, it was an imposing white building with a blue minaret. There was no movement as we approached: no cars, no dogs, nothing. James stood up in the turret, using his night-sight to look for Barry.

Then we heard machine-gun fire to our rear right. I traversed the turret and raked the ground with a burst from the chain gun before focusing on the muzzle flashes with my Raven sight and firing again. The flashes vanished. 'Target stop,' said James.

He had summoned help on the battalion network and we were

joined by two Warriors – including Zero Alpha, our CO's vehicle – and a couple of Challenger 2 tanks. We spotted a shape on the ground and James guided a Warrior towards it. Two men ran to pick it up. A pair of arms and legs flopped down.

'He's dead, isn't he, sir?'

'I very much think so,' replied James.

Barry Stephen was in the mortar platoon. A good guy. He had been disappointed when an injury stopped him from finishing his Junior Brecon training and promoting to corporal. He wasn't one of the bevvy monsters and I never had any disciplinary issues with him. He was always keen to get home, when he could, to his wife and kids. I had lost another man from Charlie Company. I felt like vomiting.

James radioed the CO. 'You should head back now, sir,' he said. 'We'll provide protective cover.' Lee reversed our Warrior as the other vehicles began to withdraw. While traversing the turret to stay facing the mosque, I spotted a two-man RPG team. One knelt down with the launcher on his shoulder and the other stood beside him to load the rounds. The shooter was facing towards Zero Alpha. I put the armed selector switch on, pressed down on the foot-firing switch and destroyed him. The other guy ran away and I traversed the turret slightly to catch him.

'Target destroyed. Target stop,' said James. I cursed quietly; I wanted to kill the other RPG guy. However, I pushed the armed selector switch back to off and the green light on the chain-gun control panel lit up.

Zero Alpha had gone and we were the only ones left. Lee was panicking down the intercom. 'Sir, they're all over the place. We've got to get the fuck out of here.'

'Calm down,' I urged him, traversing the turret away from the mosque. 'Move out but keep a steady pace. Don't overtake anyone and make sure we stay at the back.'

NINE

'What Have You Done?'

We stopped at VCP2 to check that everyone was OK and then pressed on to the Crown Jewels. James stood up in the turret and surveyed the road, using the weapon sight detached from his SA80 rifle. We were the last back and a dark confusion of vehicles blocked the path to our hastily abandoned gear.

James jumped out to get an update on Barry Stephen. He gave me his weapon sight and I stood on the gunner's seat with my torso in full view above the turret. I loosened my chinstrap to shout down to the men below. Could we go around the inner perimeter? Someone said that we could but we would have to go through a berm, a defensive ditch.

'Can anyone guide us through?'

Sergeant Albert Thomson – 'Tommo' – stepped forward. 'Sure,' he said, 'I've got a cylume.'

'Sergeant Thomson is the ground commander,' I told Lee on the intercom.

Slowly we moved forward, following the blue light from Tommo's cylume as he walked backwards a few yards ahead of us. The light wobbled and vanished as he stepped into the berm.

'What the fuck's he doing?' I asked Lee, who had halted the Warrior.

'Must have fallen over.'

Then we saw the light again and inched forward. With my left hand, I removed my goggles, dropping them into the exterior plastic bin while with my right hand I gripped the rim of the turret.

Suddenly, with unexpected force, we dipped into the ditch. I felt the nose-cone hit the earth and was knocked forwards and backwards against the edge of the turret. The force jolted my loosened helmet and detached my earpiece. I heard a noise and saw that Lee had switched on the Warrior's headlights.

Jesus! Had we crushed Tommo?

My helmet came off as I pushed myself out of the turret and jumped down to the ground. Christine dipped into the sand at a 45-degree angle and Tommo lay face down on the opposite slope. Blood seeped from the back of his left thigh.

'Medic!' I heard shouts. Someone was kneeling over Tommo. I was stunned. What had happened? It must have been the chain gun. Lee confirmed that he had heard the gun fire and seen the tracer. But how? I couldn't have fired it standing up in the turret. And I'd switched it off earlier.

Knowing too well the ferocity of the gun, I feared the worst for Tommo.

Then James was beside me. 'What happened?' he asked.

'The gun must have fired. That vehicle must be isolated and inspected. No one can use it,' I said robotically.

James climbed inside the turret to check that the gun was switched off.

Tommo was stretchered away.

The commanding officer, Lieutenant Colonel Mike Riddell-Webster, appeared. 'What have you done?' he asked.

I said nothing. It wasn't even in my mind to protest my innocence. What do you mean, what have *I* done? I thought.

• • •

With Mark Calder acting as ground commander, Lee drove the Warrior out of the berm and back to our original position. I followed them on foot and sat on an exposed sand dune, looking down on

Christine. She had just killed one of my men. I didn't expect Tommo to survive the chain gun's terrible assault. Two men lost in one day. It was unthinkable.

Davey Bruce, the Black Watch RSM, appeared. Saying nothing, he sat down beside me and put an arm around my shoulder. I drew comfort from his solidarity and then we both got up and I went to speak to my crew, who were sitting around listlessly. 'Best get into your sleeping bags and get some rest,' I said.

I returned to the sand dune and stayed there all night. People from the REME came to have a look at the Warrior, first Lance Corporal Shoemaker and then Corporal Frost, who had worked on Christine when she had broken down at Barnsley. They took turns climbing into the turret with torches in their mouths.

The morning sun's hot glow failed to dissolve my despondency. The crew tried to cheer me up over breakfast.

'Everyone knows the chain gun's a crazy fucker,' said Lee.

'Aye, and the whole bloody Warrior,' added Mark, reminding me of the electric shocks that he kept getting from the radio system.

Then Jock Crowe, the regimental signals warrant officer, came through with a sliver of hope. 'Tommo's alive,' he said, 'but he's badly hurt. We just have to hope and pray.'

He added, 'Rachel's here.'

'What?'

'She's just brought a prisoner for interrogation.'

I hurried to see her in the briefing tent beside the command tent. She put her arms around me, sobbing, and I hugged her with all the power left in me. We sat and talked.

'I've been at VCP2,' she said.

'Holy shit! Were you there last night?'

'Yes. Were you? I heard that someone from Charlie Company was dead but I didn't know who.'

Rachel had herself nearly been killed by a bullet fired during a shoot 'n' scoot attack. It had splattered sand in her face as she lay in her sleeping bag. I had almost lost her.

I told her about Tommo. 'They think I shot him.' Riddell-Webster's words were lodged in my head.

'I'm so sorry,' she said, squeezing my hand. 'But you've got to try and put this out of your mind and carry on.'

As a military policewoman, Rachel knew only too well what could be in store for me.

I left her and went to James. 'Let's get ourselves a replacement Warrior,' I said. 'We don't want another accident.'

But we were stunned by the response from Captain Clarke of the REME. 'In my professional opinion the vehicle is safe to use,' he said.

'No it fucking isn't,' said James. 'It needs to be properly inspected. You should get MSG [the Land Accident Investigation Team's mobile support group] up here to look at it.'

'It's unsafe for them to come,' said Clarke.

I couldn't believe my ears. Food and water were being delivered to us along a secure corridor from Kuwait. Why couldn't the LAIT come by the same route to investigate this serious, life-threatening problem? That was their job. I felt that we shouldn't be relying on a quick night-time examination by REME men with torches.

'Are you telling me you honestly believe this vehicle is safe?' James fumed. He listed some of the times when it had broken down or given us shocks or when the chain gun had stalled in battle.

'I am satisfied that my armourer and electrician found no fault that caused the gun to fire. It was human error,' said Clarke. 'The CO agrees with me,' he added.

I knew I had to hide my rage. The men of Charlie Company looked to me for inspiration and I couldn't go around moping bitterly. Their lives were at stake.

We were told to take an intelligence officer to Bridge 4 – where Barry Stephen had been heading the previous day before he took a fatal wrong turning. I offered Rachel a lift back to VCP2 and she squashed into the back with the IO and the crew.

Lee switched on Christine's engine and I switched off the armament armed switch (AAS), cutting the power to the chain gun. I had never done this before. We were ordered to keep the

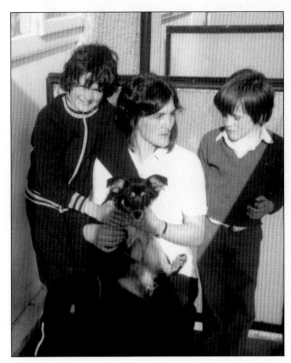

Aged nine with Mum, Bob and our dog, Judy. We had just moved into our own flat on the Durham Estate. However, our happiness was about to be destroyed by the explosion of violence inflicted on us by Terry.

Leading the parade of the new junior NCOs as cadre sergeant major in 1987, in front of the battalion and Lieutenant Colonel Alastair Irwin, who had just promoted me to lance corporal.

On the steps of Old College, Sandhurst, with the Sovereign's Platoon 1999. Angus McAfee and I are seated. Corky Corcoran is over my left shoulder and Richie Forsyth is in the front row, second from right (© Tempest Photography).

Myself, General Sir Alistair Irwin, adjutant general, and Lieutenant Colonel Mike Riddell-Webster, commanding officer, setting the regimental colours in Fallingbostel, 2002.

The Savages in Pristina, Kosovo, June 2002, outside the Olympic stadium, which had been destroyed during the fighting. Ed Jones was our company commander.

Bridge 3 at the Shatt al-Arab, 5 April 2003. James and I having a brew whilst waiting for the battle group to join us. We were to launch them into attack formation for the invasion of Basra.

During the armoured procession into Basra, 6 April. The crowd had run up the road to attack the crew of a downed Cobra helicopter. Note the orange mine tape, which the civilians were told not to cross, and the barrel of my Rarden cannon pointed directly at them.

James and I in the Iraqi army barracks nicknamed 'Shitsville', 8 April, with captured enemy weapons and looted dollars. Prisoners were being interrogated by the recce platoon in the building behind us.

Privates King and Campbell of the mortar platoon involved in FIBUA in Basra. Note the AK-47s: at times, the enemy's weapons were used when we ran out of ammo.

Sergeant Jim Mathieson and his men. The mortar platoon were heavily involved in fighting throughout Op Telic 1 and very badly affected by the loss of Lance Corporal Barry Stephen.

Destroyed T-54/55 enemy tanks on the outskirts of Basra. The British Challenger 2 was extremely effective in a one-on-one situation.

In front of my Warrior, Zero Bravo, aka 'Christine'. The blackened areas on the nose-cone are RPG strike marks.

Our initial entry into Camp Stephen did not go as planned. As James led the armour in, he attempted to drive over the roundabout and this is what happened. I hounded him for it – what a laugh.

Camp Stephen – the rebuild. Me with, from left to right, War and Muhammad, both builders, Wahlid, our interpreter and Talib, Mr Fix-It.

Me with worry beads, shemagh and dishdash – the gear used in the undercover assault on the steel factory. Underneath I wore an assault vest, with pistol and rifle concealed.

With the female interpreters who were used in the very successful confidential telephone line. To the right is Wahlid's brother, another excellent interpreter.

Jim Davidson visited the Savages in Camp Stephen and was warmly welcomed by the Jocks; even I was glad to see him. He insisted on seeing my captured-weapons armoury, the largest of its kind in Basra.

Jimmy Russell, far left, and his boys from the Milan platoon, the most heavily armed sub-unit in the battle group. These were the boys to call if you had sniper trouble.

On our way to the Iran–Iraq border, we stopped at a bombed Iraqi commando barracks. I am standing next to the only wall left, pointing at an amazingly accurate intelligence map, with all our major units plotted correctly. The enemy were not to be underestimated.

Standing at the entrance to Camp Stephen on 20 June 2003, the day I left Iraq and the Black Watch. Note the plaque that Talib was able to produce for us. The mortar platoon has kept it to this day.

Standing with Warren Lister in front of Zero Bravo outside the military appeal court in Aldershot, June 2004. The case was still ongoing when this photo was taken and I didn't know how it would turn out.

AAS on at all times to compensate for another fault. We had to activate a different switch, the armed selector switch (ASS), before firing the chain gun with our foot. But the gun had shot Tommo with the ASS switched off. A proper investigation of the Warrior had been blocked and the problem might recur. I was taking no chances. James saw what I had done but said nothing.

As we drove out of the Crown Jewels, I felt a tapping on my leg and looked down to see Rachel's hand outstretched with a note. It said: 'You are the bravest man I have ever known. Be strong. I love you very much. Rachel.' Inside the note was a crumpled 250-dinar bill with the image of Saddam Hussein crossed out.

At VCP2, I dismounted and walked Rachel to her tent. 'What's the significance of the dinars?' I asked.

'An Iraqi gave it to me when I got here,' she said. 'He came up and kissed my hand. Then he took out the note, crossed out the picture of Saddam and ground it under his heel. Maybe it'll keep you safe.'

We cuddled again. We were not meant to display these emotions in war but it was difficult not to under the circumstances. In the week since we'd last met, I had killed a lot of people and seen one of my men killed and another seriously injured. A week is a long time on active service.

Bridge 4 was a suspension bridge stretching for about 800 metres across the Shatt al-Arab. On the Basra side, the enemy was entrenched at a university complex. They were making use of a tunnel system to pop out unexpectedly at points along the riverbank and shower us with mortars.

As we approached the bridge, we saw that the road was cluttered with bombed technicals and corpses, which were often charred, with horribly bared teeth. The dead were a mixture of militiamen, incinerated in their jeeps by our forces, and fleeing Iraqi civilians, killed by regime loyalists. We stopped at a concrete compound with a tin roof, the operations base for B Company and the SAS. The IO, a tall, wavy-haired guy who chain-smoked flamboyantly, went to swap intelligence.

Major Lindsay MacDuff was in charge. By now, he was at least wearing proper armour. I learned that his men had been involved in another blue on blue. Early that morning, Black Watch tanks from B Company had killed two British soldiers when they mistakenly fired on tanks from the Queen's Royal Lancers.

Frank Mason was at Bridge 4. He already knew about the incident with Tommo. Word travels fast on the army radio network. 'Are you OK?' he asked.

'Sure,' I replied, feeling awful.

An Iraqi former brigadier was walking about with handcuffed prisoners. He was middle-aged, wearing a Saddam-style moustache and American combats. He had defected before the war and settled his family in Britain before returning to assist our operations. He spoke perfect English and told me that he had been trained at Sandhurst.

James knew most of the SAS guys at the base. They wore US combats and pistols, and I noticed a few bottles of beer lying around their room. This was something I wouldn't permit in wartime but these guys had their own modus operandi. They were mounting raids into Basra and dropping off mobile phones for potential turncoats in the Republican Guard. The officers were being tempted with large bribes to abandon their men. This often worked and if it didn't, the phones enabled us to track their movements. The special-forces guys had stashed boxes full of captured AK-47s, which they planned to distribute to Saddam-hating Shia groups. The plan of the hour was to surround Basra and encourage an uprising.

Suddenly, the ground shook as we came under mortar fire. We could see women and children running across the bridge, cowering, their hands up, and then turning back to Basra rather than running into the path of the explosions.

The IO was ready and we all clambered back aboard Christine. Lee reversed her and I rotated the turret so that our guns faced the enemy across the water. I switched on the AAS. 'Fuck sakes!' I yelled down the intercom as my hand was thrown back by a painful electric shock. This Warrior, I thought. It could have killed Tommo and now it was leaving us undefended as mortars exploded all around us. We withdrew at speed.

TEN

Liberation

On 25 March, D Company raided a house in Az Zubayr that our intelligence told us was a hideout for local leaders of the Ba'ath Party. The company used a Warrior to smash into the building. All the occupants bar one were killed. The survivor was taken for interrogation.

The next day, the company seized a prison in the town and we joined them there. It was a single-storey grey building with barred windows, infested with flies and stinking of rotten flesh and excrement. We learned that it had been built on a stagnant sewer. Charlie Company set up in a room with a large communal bath. Above the bath and bolted to the ceiling were three large metal rings. Positioned beside the bath was a big tree trunk treated with linseed oil or grease and scarred with heavy cuts. It was like a chopping block. The place reminded me of the horrors I'd seen in Spandau Prison. The prison was to be our base for several days. We were happy to get out on operations. I preferred the discomfort of sleeping upright in the Warrior to bedding down in a torture chamber.

We went to recover the missing Royal Engineers' Land Rover. Badly burned, it was a poignant reminder of the plight of those poor guys. We knew they had been alive when they were pulled from the vehicle – but where were they now? We secured the area and used the Warrior to drag the Land Rover out of view. At least then the enemy couldn't gloat over it.

James and I took on a role as special-forces liaison officers. In the coming weeks, we would assist the SAS and other units on several operations. This made sense, given James's background in the special forces. Our first assignment was to take an Iraqi informer around Az Zubayr looking for those involved in kidnapping the Engineers. He was a young man in a black tracksuit with a bum-fluff moustache and a slimy demeanour. We disguised him in a military shemagh (the traditional headscarf, sand-coloured for camouflage) and my helmet and put him up in the turret with James. I sat in the back with the SAS while the informer discreetly pointed out various houses. We spent three days doing this and eagerly awaited news of arrests.

While we were out on the road, the radio crackled with the news that the prison was under sniper attack. Then Jimmy Russell, the second in command of our Milan platoon, resolved the problem with an anti-tank missile. He killed the sniper and demolished the building from which he was shooting. We also heard reports of a major engagement involving the Royal Scots Dragoon Guards. It turned into the British Army's biggest tank battle since the Second World War. Fourteen Iraqi tanks were destroyed: a superb achievement. Their antique T-54s and T-55s – cast offs from the Soviet Union – were no match for our state-of-the-art Challenger 2s.

At the prison, we took delivery of five tankers of water and food from Kuwait and the locals were told to come to us for supplies. At times, our men had to firmly contain crowds on the verge of rioting but these hiccups didn't feature in the British press. There was a widespread belief among the soldiers that the aid handout had more to do with creating some good photo opportunities than it did with alleviating any genuine need. A few days later, we were ordered, as part of the 'hearts and minds' operation, to replace our helmets with tam-o'-shanters on patrol. One of the Jocks summed up the general view: 'What a bag of bollocks.' Some felt that this requirement, at a time when we were still very much at risk, was part of a PR exercise that seemed to have been planned with medals in mind.

On the night of 29 March, we went to refuel at a concentration point on the edge of town and James and I decided to stretch out and get some proper sleep under Christine's tracks. Shattered after many nights of emergency battle sleep, I paid scant attention when the now familiar noise of mortars started up. James, however, sat bolt upright like Frankenstein's monster.

'Is that affecting us, Sergeant Major?'

'Nah,' I replied sleepily.

The next round hit the truck beside us, peppering the Warrior with shrapnel and showering me with glass from the lights. People started screaming. We scrambled back inside Christine. The men in the truck were badly hurt and casevaced home. I discovered that Tommo had been sent home too. He had survived but one of his legs had had to be amputated. Nobody discussed it with me again for some time but it weighed heavily on my mind.

Charlie Company became a bit fragmented during these days. 'Rent a Savage' was the order of the day. As weapons specialists, our men were often bolted on to operations by other companies. We maintained cohesion through regular orders meetings with all our 'heads of shed', the commanders from all the units, including me. James relayed information from the CO orders meetings and I focused on discipline and morale. In time of war, it was more important than ever for me to live up to my reputation (articulated in an appraisal report) for keeping the Jocks in 'a vice-like grip, with a touch of compassion'.

There were many raids into Basra, including one, led by the CO, that destroyed a statue of Saddam and a TV tower. However, it became clear that the hoped-for Shia insurgency was not going to materialise. This was probably because the Shias felt a sense of betrayal dating back to 1991, when the Americans hadn't supported them during their uprising at the end of the first Gulf War. Saddam had sent Ali Hassan al-Majid, the notorious 'Chemical Ali', to wreak a terrible vengeance. Tens of thousands were tortured and killed. This time round, the Shias were keeping their heads down and our allied forces still faced fierce resistance from the Fedayeen and other government loyalists.

On 3 April, the Black Watch handed control of Az Zubayr to the Duke of Wellington's Regiment and we relocated to nearby Shaibah airfield, which was to become the main coalition HQ. James and I were sent to set up a recce group at Bridge 3, two or three miles from Basra. For the next two days, we watched as British and American air strikes pulverised targets in the city. Waves of attack helicopters showered missiles down on it, leaving heavy palls of smoke. Huge JDAM (Joint Direct Attack Munition) precision bombs thundered as they razed buildings. Meanwhile, our group marked out the ground around Bridge 3 for the Black Watch Battle Group to form up before making a full-scale assault on the city.

On the night of 5 April, Riddell-Webster briefed me on the agreed order of march. It was the first time he had spoken to me since the incident with Tommo and we restricted the conversation to the impending operation.

At 0230 hours, I waved off the first group of Challenger 2s as they moved across the bridge towards Basra's glowing sky. We sat in Christine waiting for our turn to move and listening to radio reports. One exchange sticks in my mind.

'An Iraqi male has climbed onto the turret of the call sign in front,' came a report from a tank crew leading the assault. 'Permission to engage him.'

'Is he a threat?' asked the CO.

'Yes.'

'Remove him.'

Then the sound of a short burst of gunfire.

'Target removed.'

At last, Zero Bravo joined the armoured procession, crossing the bridge and heading along an open road into the city. The earth was shaking from the repeated air strikes. Standing up in the turret at first light, I noticed a US Cobra attack helicopter hovering above us and firing into the city. 'I can't believe how still he is,' I said to James. Then we heard the tutting of a Duschka anti-aircraft gun and the Cobra screamed as if in pain, lurching erratically forward and landing heavily on the road about a kilometre in front of us.

We were the only call sign within reach, so we rushed forward. I was horrified to see a crowd suddenly materialise on the far side of the Cobra. The mob was closer to the Americans than we were and, through my times-eight sight, it appeared that some of them were carrying petrol cans. 'Get a move on!' I yelled to Lee. 'We could have a Mogadishu on our hands.' As the driver hit our top speed of about 80 kph, I recalled grim scenes from the film *Black Hawk Down*, an account of the US military intervention in Somalia in 1993, during which American helicopters were shot down, landing amidst crowds of hostile militiamen.

The Cobra crew had jumped out of the cockpit and taken up firing positions. We raced past them and halted about 100 metres ahead, in front of an excited crowd about 200-strong, with boys at the front and men at the back. They stopped jumping about when I switched on the chain gun and put a burst into the ground.

James got out, taking a roll of mine tape with him, which he used to create a line across the road. 'If anyone crosses this line,' he told them in Arabic, 'we will shoot him dead.' He went to talk to the grateful Yanks. Another Cobra hovered overhead. If we weren't here, I thought, they would probably just open up on the crowd. Then a Challenger 2 tank pulled up behind the crowd, ruling out the possibility that someone might throw a petrol bomb and run off. The mob melted away, more Americans came and we pressed on to the city.

We had converted ten Warriors into ambulances at Bridge 3 but these proved unnecessary. As the battle group crashed into Basra, it encountered only pockets of stern resistance. Our air raids had been pretty effective.

When Zero Bravo reached the city, it dawned on me that most of the local traffic was made up of people taking advantage of the collapse of the old regime. Busy gangs with pick-up trucks and horse-drawn carts were emptying government buildings, shops and even houses. We were under orders not to interfere with the looting.

Apart from the 'Ali Babas' (the term the Iraqis used for 'criminal'), few people were out on the streets. Some waved, while others just eyeballed us. It was an uncertain introduction to a city still smoking from the impact of our huge bombs. Some houses as well as government buildings were now rubble and I feared for the families who had lived in them. Every 200 metres, we passed sandbagged bunkers. They were silent but I wondered when we would come under attack.

We stopped at a hospital and went into a ward divided by a curtain. On one side lay the patients, while on the other weapons and green uniforms had been hastily abandoned. The enemy wasn't shy of hiding behind the sick and injured. Then we raided a barracks, where we found more discarded gear and some warm cups of coffee in a briefing room. It was frustrating; we could almost taste the foe. We were in the mood for a punch-up but had to make do with taking their weapons outside into the street and driving over them.

We pushed on, past a couple of burned technicals with bodies hanging out of them, and stopped at the SIS (secret intelligence services) building, the headquarters of the Mukhabarat, Saddam's feared secret police. Much of this large compound had been JDAM-ed but, behind its high wall, there were enough intact structures for the CO to set up his battalion HQ and be joined by Delta Company.

Charlie Company was left with the task of finding itself a base. Many of our men spent their first night in Basra sleeping out in their Warriors. Several of the Jocks felt that we were being reckless moving into Basra beyond our agreed line of exploitation. We had pushed on further than originally intended, which meant that we became very thin on the ground.

On 8 April we carried out more clearance patrols in the area around the new HQ. The Fedayeen were still bobbing about and we turned a corner to be greeted by the rattle of an AK-47. 'It's from that flat over there,' I said, spotting movement in a window on the first floor of a little flat-roofed block.

Leaving two men to provide cover in depth, James and I charged up the stairs and kicked in the apartment's front door. A woman cowered with her two children on the living room floor, screaming in terror. She was young and pretty, wearing a traditional headscarf. At this stage, most of Basra's women were not wearing burkhas, although in the wake of the invasion religious extremism prospered. 'No Ali Baba, no Ali Baba.' Her husband repeated this mantra and pointed to an open window at the back, indicating that the gunman had fled. We left them in peace.

We started clearing houses that had been identified as a potential threat to the HQ. In one, we found a stock of RPGs, home-made explosives and six walkie-talkies. We destroyed the RPGs, put the explosives in an 'incident pit' for safe detonation and distributed the radios for vehicle-to-vehicle communications. These patrols reminded me of Northern Ireland. In the coming weeks, we would draw heavily on those experiences of policing volatile streets and tackling 'hit-and-run' bombers and gunmen.

Meanwhile, I was determined to bring the Savages back together under one roof. This would improve the quality of our endangered lives and enable me to keep a grip on them. We might be in the Wild West but I didn't want them to become cowboys. On the night of the 8th, we took over a barracks where the corridors were full of discarded Iraqi uniforms, so much so that the doors were at first jammed with abandoned helmets. The place was filthy, overrun by mad dogs and mosquitoes. The Jocks christened it 'Shitsville'.

James and I tried to ignore the canine chorus and grab some sleep in a first-floor room. 'Fuck this,' said James eventually. He got up, cocked his rifle and went downstairs. A shot rang out, followed by a dreadful whining. Back he came.

'Get one?'

'Sergeant Major, it was two dogs with one round.'

In the morning, I spoke to Corporal Pratt of the recce platoon. 'Tell your guys to get rid of the dogs,' I said. 'I don't care how you do it.' To my surprise, he went to pull a pile of captured AK-47s from his vehicle. At least he wasn't wasting my bullets.

We would have to move on. The wall surrounding the barracks was too low. Locals kept looking in on us: one minute it was an inquisitive kid but the next it might be a gunman. We kept scouting for alternatives.

We raided a nearby school and found stocks of grenades and a Duschka anti-aircraft machine gun in the playground. Hospitals and schools all seemed to be fair game for the enemy. It hardened the hearts of my men. Then we found a school that seemed to offer an ideal base. It was in good nick, had four floors, high walls and a huge concrete playground where we could shelter our vehicles. The place initially seemed empty but on our second recce we found a group of men hiding in a room. Dressed in suits and ties, they weren't militiamen. The head teacher spoke to us in good English. 'We have been protecting the school from looters,' he said. 'If you wish, we will offer it to you. But that would deny the children their education.'

'No, you keep the school,' said James, 'and we'll try to help you by stepping up our patrols.' We kept our word and were pleased when the school did safely reopen.

Everywhere, the thieving was escalating. I'd had enough of turning a blind eye and got my senior NCOs together. 'If you see it, stop it,' I said. The Savages weren't averse to intervening with a cuff around the ear or a rifle up the nostril. Soon, the official line changed, too, and we were all told to contain the looting.

One day, Sergeant Jim Mathieson of the mortar platoon was out on patrol when he heard a sudden explosion. He set up a snap vehicle checkpoint, stopping a car whose passengers were armed and had a bag full of dollars.

'We just withdrew the money,' said one of the men, shrugging his shoulders.

'Aye,' said Jim as he took them into custody, 'you withdrew it with a fucking grenade.'

He gave me the loot, which I put in a sandbag and stashed in the back of the Warrior. We went around checking more of the banks. Almost all of them had had their vaults blown open.

ELEVEN

Camp Stephen

My primary concern at this point was to find somewhere decent for my men to stay. For almost three weeks, we'd lived relentlessly on the edge: risking death, sometimes killing, never relaxing and sleeping in our vehicles or in the likes of the torture chamber. This was unavoidable at the height of war but now we had captured Basra, it was time for the Savages to enjoy a whiff of normality.

After three nights at Shitsville, one of our patrols brought good tidings. They had been monitoring Chemical Ali's former barracks on the outskirts of the city. It looked big enough for us and there was no sign of a military presence. James and I went with the anti-tank platoon to seize the barracks. It was at the end of a road full of big empty homes. We crashed through the entrance and found only some families of vanished soldiers. We told them to leave.

The infrastructure was gutted – toilets, showers, lights and furniture all gone – and rubbish was strewn everywhere. But I knew that this would make an ideal home for Charlie Company. The structures were intact and there was plenty of room. We were surrounded by a high wall with guard towers on each corner: Chemical Ali had evidently wanted to see his enemies coming. We had no immediate neighbours now that his cronies had abandoned their nearby mansions. This could be a reasonably secure place to return to after a hard day's soldiering. I was delighted to discover that there was still a water supply. It wasn't drinkable but it would do for washing.

I organised a big clean-up. The place was to be pristine before everyone moved in. We didn't want a free-for-all, with the Jocks fighting for the best spaces, so James and I carefully allocated a room to each of the four platoons and the REME. Then we summoned the men in groups and sent them to their new quarters.

When you drove through the gates, you came to a little roundabout linked to a circular tarmac road that ran around the interior of the barracks. James ordered Lee to drive Christine straight across it but she stuck fast in the soft earth. We got another Warrior to drag her out as our embarrassed commander hurried to our new ops room. The next day, I saw that the tarmac was being torn up by the armoured vehicles. I ordered the engineers to build an eight-foot sand berm, creating a well-protected parking space in front of barracks, with one entry point manned by two sentries.

The day we moved in, we received our first visitors. Ali Babas were robbing their workplace – could we help? We took the Warrior across a river at the back of the barracks and on to a big warehouse that looked like a B&Q store. It stocked clothing, farm machinery and all sorts of other goods. Close to a railway line, it seemed to be part of an import and export business.

I approached a car inside the warehouse and dropped in a phosphorous smoke grenade. Spluttering passengers abandoned the vehicle, which was loaded with goodies, and the other looters paid attention to us as we brandished our weapons. Then a bullet whacked a brick wall two inches above my head. I ran with James out of the warehouse and across some ground to a little factory. A security guard protested his ignorance of any gunman, even after I gave him a Black Watch throat rash by gripping him firmly around the neck.

At least we stopped the looting, though. The workers came back to fix the gates to the warehouse, although their bosses had vanished and they didn't know when they would next get paid.

We expanded our improvised policing responsibilities to cover an area of the city called al-Hayaniyah. 'It's a vast Shia district,' said James. He'd been briefed by the CO but intelligence on the ground was poor and no one knew much about the place. 'The regime really hammered them after 1991 and they've become self-supporting.' There was only one way to find out more about the place, so we set off on the 15-minute drive to our new beat, leaving the Warriors behind and taking stripped-down Land Rovers. I wore a helmet, a combat assault vest and my skydiving goggles, to keep out the dust.

If you can imagine Shangri-La, al-Hayaniyah was the opposite. Endless rows of grim tenement blocks were interspersed with houses like fortresses and waste ground awash with rubbish. The roads were often just hardened earth with open sewers running down the middle, where men and boys openly defecated. It was an ants' nest of activity, full of Arab Arthur Daleys, with street-side truck hire, donkeys for sale and all manner of business. It seemed as if everything looted from Basra had ended up in al-Hayaniyah. Countless stolen vehicles were filled with stashed booty. We kept seeing big bundles of looted steel rods about the place; guys were out in front of their houses with blowtorches using the steel rods to build high gates, fences and the like, presumably to order.

We went to introduce ourselves to the officers at the police station in the adjacent district of al-Jamariah. An angry crowd had gathered outside, throwing stones.

'Why are the locals turning on them?' I wondered aloud.

'I suspect they're corrupt bastards,' said James.

Even though the station was under attack, the head cop bristled at our appearance. In a basement room, I found an old man tied to a chair with blood on his nose and cuts on his hands. Like a whipped dog, he looked at me imploringly. I didn't care what he might have done and cut him loose.

'Ali Baba, Ali Baba!' a policeman protested aggressively, and I flattened him with a punch.

'Don't like these punters,' I told James.

We went up on the roof to survey the protestors and a rock just missed me. 'Get me that guy,' I ordered a couple of men from the mortar platoon. They went out and some of the crowd grabbed the culprit and handed him over. He was hauled up. I theatrically picked up the rock, then pointed to his plasticuffed hands and shook my head. We handed him over to the cops.

The police didn't want us there and the locals didn't want the police. We had to try to fill the vacuum. Without realising the scale of the challenge, I resolved that Charlie Company would impose some semblance of law and order. But we would need allies.

James and I went on a foot patrol, followed by clusters of boisterous kids smiling and yelling, 'How are you?'

The two of us stopped at a street stall. 'Chai,' said James and we were given cups of sweet tea in espresso-sized glasses. A small, friendly crowd gathered. They seemed fascinated by our tam-o'-shanters.

'Hello, sirs, how are you?' A tall, thin guy of about 30 spoke to us in perfect English and shook our hands. 'Do you need interpreters?'

'Absolutely,' I said.

'I will be your interpreter. I have a masters degree in English and used to teach it at the university.'

'Are you working now?'

'No. The university closed down when the war started. I have no money and my family is very hungry.'

'We can pay you a dollar a day.'

'That will be very good. Tell me what you want me to do.'

Wahlid came back to our camp for a briefing. He became the first of our 49 local employees and the head of our group of 36 interpreters. He was a gem, highly intelligent and socially at ease. He could just as easily joke with the Jocks as pretend to be deferential to the CO.

One day, he took us to his home. I was shocked to discover that he lived with his wife and two children in just one room with a hole in the corner for a toilet. 'He's working for us. I can't have him living like that,' I said to James. The next time Wahlid came to the camp, I took him to the nearest of the abandoned mansions.

'Who lived here?' I asked.

'Someone important,' he replied. 'A very bad man.'

'What do you think of the place?'

'I think it would be very good for a big family.'

When I produced the front-door keys, Wahlid burst into tears. He moved in with his wife and children, his father and his brother's family, and I got his new home connected to our electricity generator.

Wahlid introduced us to Talib. He looked like Danny DeVito in a dishdash. He was gallus. 'Hello, Meester Tam, how are you?' was his usual breezy greeting. Talib became our indispensable Mr Fix-It. He was a superb craftsman and built us bookcases, cupboards and beds. He was also a man who knew people, recruiting plumbers to install our showers and builders to extend our kitchen and dining area.

I was very proud of the showers. We had arrested a Fedayeen leader and I had taken the time to examine his washing arrangements. The water was pumped up to a tin can with a shower head attached to it. It seemed a good model and I took the contraption away for further study. But how could we afford enough shower heads, not to mention the chairs we needed for the canteen? The army had given us just $50 to kit out our camp of 200 people. We were already digging into our own pockets to buy extra food and pay the interpreters. Then I remembered the haul of money that Jim Mathieson had confiscated from the looter. I went to Christine, who was parked up now and rarely used. The sandbag was full of notes – more than $2,000. We immediately put this to good use.

Before we set up camp, my men had lived like dogs, often eating by the side of the road. Now they had proper meals. We pooled the ration packs to boil big broths and bought 200 bread rolls and fresh vegetables each day. It made a real difference to the Jocks' morale to be able to take off their helmets and eat together like humans. However, we were haunted by our camp's brutal history. It had been built by Saddam's Himmler, a beast steeped in the blood of thousands of Kurds and Shia Muslims. At the time, we thought that Chemical Ali had been killed in an air raid but he was later captured and eventually sentenced to the ultimate throat rash.

On a Sunday in late April, the regimental padre came to conduct a memorial service for Barry Stephen. I left a couple of guys on sentry duty and everyone else gathered outside for the ceremony. Two of Barry's pals read from the Bible and delivered short eulogies. They talked of the bravery of our fallen comrade – a great friend who loved his football and was an exemplary family man. Talib made us a plaque to fix to the gate. It bore the name of our home: Camp Stephen.

• • •

'What the fuck's going on?' Lieutenant Colonel Riddell-Webster had sent my friend Davey Bruce, the RSM, to complain about the tight security on our gate.

'Sorry,' I said, 'but no one gets in here with their vehicles. Not even the SAS. You can park up safely behind the berms and walk in.'

The issue had arisen when the CO had arrived to make his first visit to Camp Stephen, about a week after we'd moved in. 'What do you mean I can't drive in?' he'd shouted at the sentry who was refusing to let his cavalcade sweep in. 'I'm your commanding officer!'

It wasn't the best start and I couldn't help but wonder whether Riddell-Webster was peeved about our new home. I never heard him compliment us on our achievement, of which I was immensely proud. Left to fend for ourselves, we had managed better than most. We were, according to our SAS friends, the only unit in Basra enjoying fresh food. The camp had been a shell but we were rebuilding it, even putting in some glass to keep out the wind. Now we had flushing toilets and showers, a TV and satellite dish. In our ops room, we sat around a giant table that Talib had found for us.

On 24 April, the Secretary of State for Defence, Geoff Hoon, visited our camp. It was one month to the day since Barry Stephen's death and at 11 a.m. we were holding a one-minute silence. With perfect timing, the minister's fixers arrived at our gate at this moment, demanding to be let in. I kept them waiting. In the afternoon, Hoon came to camp with the CO and the Jocks waited in their platoon quarters to meet him after he had seen the heads of shed.

'Any questions?'

I asked him about food parcels. Many of us were getting extra food sent from home and there had been talk on the radio of families getting a free postal service.

'Well, it only costs about six pounds to post a parcel,' said our defence minister.

This response annoyed me. It struck me as glib and it was inaccurate, too. 'It cost my mother twice that much,' I said, 'and she's a pensioner.'

Then we went to see the mortar platoon – Barry Stephen's platoon – and I was shocked by the frigid reception. Not one of the Jocks stood up for the minister and he struggled to start a conversation with any of them. They were still grieving for Barry and refused to play ball. 'No photos,' whispered the press officer to the accompanying media.

Some days later, James returned downhearted from an orders meeting. 'The CO wants us to relocate to the SIS building. What do you think, Sergeant Major?'

I was fuming. Look after this place, I had promised my men, and we will not move again. 'Of course, it's up to you, sir,' I said to James, 'but the Jocks will be seriously pissed off if we have to move. That place is a shithole compared to this. It'll have a very bad effect on morale. What is the point of us moving two miles up the road?' No doubt the order was well intended but to me it just didn't make any sense.

'If you were me,' asked James, 'what would you do?'

'I would say no, sir.'

James stood firm and, through my junior NCOs, I quietly let the Jocks know this. 'Make sure you keep the camp in good order,' I told them, 'because the company commander has put his neck on the line for us.'

TWELVE

Keeping the Peace

We began to get more and more orders about the 'hearts and minds' aspect of the operation. If any weapon was fired, we must take a detailed statement. If it wasn't fired in self-defence, the man responsible would be charged. We must be cautious about crowd control and avoid offending the mullahs and tribal leaders. Our heads of shed met these orders with silence. They echoed government spin about burgeoning harmony in southern Iraq but this take on things didn't tally with our experience on the ground. The messages could be confusing, as well. It seemed contradictory to tell us to use kid gloves and at the same time to confiscate all weapons, given that it was an old Iraqi tradition to keep a gun in your house for protection.

The lifting of Saddam's curfew was another flawed move. It was meant to be popular with the ordinary people but, without a properly functioning police force, it allowed the gangsters and militias to operate under cover of darkness, particularly in the vast, lawless area of al-Hayaniyah, where our patrols were involved in almost daily skirmishes.

Soon after we set up Camp Stephen, Jules MacIlhenney, the commander of the mortar platoon, was involved in an intense firefight with ambushers who were armed with powerful PKM machine guns. His crew killed two of the attackers and found them well kitted out for battle.

'Zero tolerance,' I said to James. 'That's the only approach we can take or we'll be overrun.' He agreed and we spread the word that if we saw any criminal activity or anyone carrying a gun, we should step in and make arrests. We put up a sign outlining this policy at the camp entrance. Lots of locals were calling at the gate, sometimes with real problems and sometimes just to hang about. It was a security risk, so I had another sign made in Arabic: 'You have one minute to explain your case to us. If we then ask you to go away and you refuse to do so, we will arrest you.' One guy came to say that the camp was his house and we had stolen it. We put him in the POW cage, which was filling up rapidly, and let him go after an hour, but he kept coming back.

More worryingly, we had our first brush with a wannabe suicide bomber. Our men arrested a guy at a checkpoint wearing a bulky waistcoat under his dishdash. This was promptly placed in the incident pit outside the camp and James and I took a look. We lifted out the green chest rig and carefully opened its seven Velcro-fastened pouches. Inside each one, we found sticks of plastic explosive, with some 50-calibre rounds to create shrapnel. The rig also held three detonators. We'd all had a lucky escape.

I decided to try using a tactic from my time in Northern Ireland to reach out to the locals. Talib had installed a telephone for us, and another interpreter brought along three young women who spoke English and wanted to work for us in the camp but not on operations. We had some cards made in Arabic and English saying: 'If you see any criminal or terrorist activity, please call us.' We were the only unit in Iraq to set up a confidential hotline and the only British combat unit employing female interpreters.

One morning, Raneen, one of the phone operators, ran to me in a panic. 'A man is threatening to kill a teacher,' she said. 'He has a knife to her throat and he's already cut her.' The school was nearby and I sped to it with Jim Mathieson and three of his guys from the mortar platoon. We could see into the school building, where a man was holding a woman by the neck. In the playground, children were screaming.

When the assailant saw us he started yelling. Jim moved to the entrance, took aim and fired. We dashed in to find the teacher safe but hysterical and bleeding from a cut to her throat. The knife-man had a hole in his head. We called an ambulance for the teacher and I stopped a taxi and dumped her assailant's body on the back seat. 'Take him to hospital,' I said. Under the circumstances, it seemed the best thing to do.

Jim had saved the woman's life and, as the news spread, the volume of phone calls grew, with reports of robbery, rape and murder. We were just 200 soldiers policing a district with more than 200,000 inhabitants. Al-Hayaniyah was probably the most volatile place in Basra. It was Dodge City. Even the clergy were dodgy. One day, I stopped a convoy of three gleaming Shoguns. Inside one, a mullah in a black turban gave me the evil eye. They had no paperwork and claimed to have borrowed the vehicles. 'Look, you'd better cut the crap or I'll arrest you all,' I told them through an interpreter. When they admitted that the vehicles were stolen, I made them all get out and walk.

The Shoguns joined our collection of stolen vehicles, which were regularly picked up and taken to the Breadbasket, a British camp outside Basra. It became known that we usually had several 4x4s in our car park and one day an RMP lieutenant visited us. 'I need to commandeer a Shogun,' he said. 'We're going on a special-forces operation.' Nice try, I thought. When I introduced him to JP, the SAS commander based in our barracks, he went pink and started stuttering. It seemed that he'd only been after a nice car for himself and his boss to drive around in. 'Try that again and you'll get a slap,' I said as he went on his way.

We weren't always at loggerheads with the mullahs. James toured the mosques on a 'meet and greet' programme, going in unarmed, with me as his bodyguard. From behind my shades, I closely monitored the clerics' young followers, sometimes opening my vest to give them a flash of my pistol. It became clear that the Sunni mosques had begun to feel under siege in an overwhelmingly Shia city and we made a point of covering them on our patrols.

At the beginning of May, we called to see Abu Salem, a prominent mullah in al-Hayaniyah. He was holed up in a fire station with about 1,000 people outside chucking stones. The crowd wouldn't go even when his boys came out and shot someone dead. We found a pirate's cave inside: the place was packed with treasures such as fridge-freezers, DVD players, barrels of coiled copper wire and the ubiquitous steel rods. We knew where the wire came from because we'd seen a dead guy lying in the road, his hair standing on end. He'd been electrocuted digging up the power cables, a practice that was causing many of the power cuts that were disrupting the city.

Abu Salem told James that he was a man of peace. He preached at the local mosque and had instructed his flock to bring any stolen goods to the fire station so that, when things got back to normal, they could be returned to their rightful owners. James listened with a straight face to this horseshit. He deserved a medal just for his diplomatic skills. One of the interpreters told me a different story. Every night, he said, Abu Salem's men were driving lorry-loads of the loot to Iran, where it was sold on for hundreds of thousands of dollars.

Whatever the case, we still had an angry mob to deal with. As we stepped outside, another rock flew in my direction. I knew that if we didn't nail the problem there and then, it would turn into a barrage. I sent 'Big Tex', a colossal Canadian, with a few boys to collar the ringleader. He carried the guy back by the ankle, bashing his head along the way. 'The rock throwing must stop,' I told the Iraqi. 'Promise to leave the scene and I'll let you go.' Ten minutes later and he was at it again. This time, my boys trussed him like a chicken to the back of a Land Rover. I sent the recce platoon in with batons drawn to disperse the crowd.

Back inside, despite Abu Salem's protests, we took away a stash of AK-47s. James told him that we would make arrangements for the copper wire to be handed back to the relevant authorities.

Two days later, the gate sentry called me. 'Sir, there's an Iraqi priest to see you.' We brought Abu Salem and four of his entourage to the ops room.

'I need weapons for protection,' he said. 'People are stealing things and threatening us.'

'He very bad man,' the interpreter told me as he translated. 'He Ali Baba.'

We told the holy man no way and sent him packing.

However, when the CO next visited Camp Stephen, I was to be surprised by his stance on the matter. 'You must give Abu Salem ten guns for personal protection,' said Lieutenant Colonel Riddell-Webster.

'The man's a bandit, sir,' I protested.

'That's an order,' he replied.

There were strategic reasons for the order – it was in line with the coalition forces' policy of supporting and defending local Shia Muslims, who were anti-Ba'athist – but nonetheless it concerned me. With teeth gritted, we gathered up some AK-47s. I noted down their serial numbers and labelled them with green tape. 'We'll be checking in on you every day,' I told Abu Salem. 'You can only use them in self-defence and they mustn't be taken off the premises.'

We made sure that there was always a call sign parked outside his HQ. About ten days after we'd delivered the guns, we heard bad news. 'Contact. The fire station.' There was blood on the ground. Six people, members of a crowd throwing stones at the Ali Babas, had been shot down, their bodies dragged away by their friends. Meanwhile, Abu Salem's men had driven off with a lorry-load of goods. Four of the AK-47s were missing but Abu Salem seemed blasé about the shootings. I took the other six guns away, furious that we had been made to seem complicit in gangster violence. What would the local people think of us now?

The next time Abu Salem called at Camp Stephen, I made him wait for half an hour before I would speak to him. When I returned to Britain, I wasn't surprised to see his face on the TV news. He was egging on a big protest against our troops. Abu Salem was a follower of the influential political leader Muqtada al-Sadr and probably helped him to assemble his Mahdi militia. Under our noses, the Shia clerics and politicians were starting to build their new fiefdom, with a strong Iranian influence.

President Bush had denounced Iran as part of the 'axis of evil'. There was a strong rumour that Iraq wasn't the end of the job and that soon we would have to turn right and invade its neighbour. I remembered that once when we were practising in a Warrior simulator in Germany, a map of Iran had popped up. 'We're off to the next war,' I joked apprehensively when we were sent on a reconnaissance mission to the border. We had been ordered to find out about Iranian incursions and smuggling. We took a robust mixture of men – from the sniper, anti-tank and mortar platoons – on our trip to the unknown.

On the way, we stopped at a precision-bombed Iraqi commando barracks. Stepping over corpses, I studied a wall map of British and American military positions. It was astonishingly accurate. The enemy was ill equipped in comparison with us but it wasn't lacking in savvy.

The road to Iran was studded with charred tank hulks and the tail fins of buried rockets. These were relics of the Iran–Iraq War, a ten-year conflict that had claimed a million lives and during which Saddam Hussein was backed by Britain and the USA.

At the border, a bridge crossed the Shatt al-Arab, with checkpoints at each end. Ten Iranians guarded their side and a couple had crossed over to ours. A hundred metres before the Iraqi checkpoint was an ancient archway with faded gold carvings. We found steps leading up onto the top of the arch and I positioned my snipers there. An Iranian motorbike sped into the distance and then we heard the distinctive cough of T-54s and T-55s starting up before they made their arthritic way to the riverbank. The heavily bearded border guards had more modern gear – each carried a powerful Heckler & Koch G3 automatic rifle.

'I'll go and chat to them,' said James. 'Best avoid an incident.' As James strolled to the checkpoint with an interpreter, I ordered each of my snipers to select an Iranian target. However, the meeting turned out to be cordial. The Iranians told James that they had crossed the bridge because no one was controlling the Iraqi side. Tactically, this made sense. I suspected that it also made it easier for them to negotiate kickbacks with night-time smugglers before they crossed the border.

Increasingly, we felt the Iranian influence closer to home. Just up the road from Camp Stephen, at a junction with the main drag into the city centre, a big banner appeared on a white building that looked like a meeting hall. It had been empty when we'd arrived, probably old regime property. Now the entrance was thronging with men with long beards. 'We'd better check this out, sir,' I said to James. 'Looks like they're setting up a mad-mullah HQ on our doorstep.'

We left men from the recce platoon in a couple of Land Rovers and walked into the building. Men waved their arms at us. 'No, no, outside!' Surrounded by his young acolytes, the big chief came out to speak to us. He had a long black beard and a turban. I can't be certain but he resembled photos I have since seen of Muqtada al-Sadr, who was fast replacing Saddam as our main opponent in southern Iraq.

'We are here for peaceful religious purposes,' he told us through Wahlid. 'We are backed by the Iranian government. We want to look after the oppressed Shia people and promote sharia law.' James retorted that we were the legal authority until a new Iraqi administration was in place.

He spoke in measured tones but I noticed that tall, muscular men of military age were hemming us in. One of them stabbed his finger at my boss and I raised my rifle. 'Tell them,' I said to a nervous-looking Wahlid, 'that the next person to make a move towards the commander gets shot dead.' The finger-pointer stepped back and apologised but the faces surrounding us were glowing with hatred.

I spoke briefly on the radio and then said to Wahlid, 'Tell the crowd to take a look over their shoulders.' My men were standing up in their Land Rovers, pointing machine guns and rifles in our direction.

As we left, Wahlid asked, 'Do you know what the banner says?'

'All you need is love?'

'British infidel invaders get out of Iraq!'

I had the banner taken down and we reported the incident to HQ. We were told to observe and monitor but to keep our distance.

• • •

Rachel was based at the RMP headquarters and, along with other military police officers, she began to assist us with some operations. Sometimes, it could be a big help having a female officer on the job. We were getting dozens of complaints from Sunnis that their houses had been stolen by Shias. We spoke to our interpreters and to the neighbours, usually finding that the Sunni claims were true. Then we had to ease out one family, often with young children, to let another move back in. It wasn't pleasant and Rachel helped to defuse these situations.

One day when Rachel was with us, we got a contact report telling us a soldier had shot a man at a petrol station that we were approaching. In a land rich in oil, there were petrol shortages. The strict rationing that coalition forces were enforcing at the pumps was unpopular. This situation was a disappointment to us, as the Savages' beat included an oil refinery that we carefully guarded to ensure continued production. We swung into the forecourt and found a corpse on the ground, shot through the chest. It was the first time Rachel had seen a dead body. This surprised me, as I had seen so many in the past month that it was almost routine for me. We learned that the driver had been yelling that an attendant wouldn't give him extra juice. When a Jock spoke to him, the driver had grabbed him around the neck and put his foot down, dragging the soldier along and bashing him against a pillar. The Jock had managed to manoeuvre and fire his rifle. Rachel took statements and the authorities agreed that the soldier had acted in self-defence.

I frequently took James to his 5 p.m. orders meeting with the CO and then drove to the RMP HQ, which was next door to B Company, for protection. This gave me and Rachel an hour together before I collected James. It was a delight to chat about peaceful things over cups of tea. We talked about our June leave and I used the Internet access to book us a holiday cottage on Skye. It was something good to look forward to.

We also spoke about the visits to Camp Stephen that had been made by the RMP's Special Investigation Branch (SIB). They hadn't spoken to me but I knew that they were taking statements from people who had witnessed Tommo getting shot by my Warrior.

'What happens next?' I wondered.

'Keep me informed,' she said, 'and I'll help you if I can.'

Rachel was responsible for establishing a new port and maritime police service. It was a weighty task – dealing with the existing police and sorting out uniforms, boats and finances – but she tackled it with her customary aplomb. In her spare time, she was sorting out a bomb-damaged school next door to the RMP HQ. She worked with the women teachers, securing a £50,000 grant to get the building fixed and redecorated, and even went around painting the place on her own. It bothered me that she was putting herself at risk and, when I could, I accompanied her with a rifle.

When Tony Blair visited Basra on 29 May, he dropped in at the reopened school. As *The Independent* reported:

> [Blair] made his first call of the day to the Kahdija al-Kubra primary school, restored and redecorated with UK money. Schools such as these are said to have been used by the Ba'athists to store weapons; Mr Blair used it in the manner of a campaigning politician. As he was surrounded by swarms of youngsters in the school yard, he hoisted up into his arms one boy, who landed him a loud kiss on the cheek.

The prime minister sent Rachel a congratulatory letter. Unfortunately, though, this stirred up jealousy among some of her colleagues.

On one trip to see Rachel, I heard some disturbing rumours about the investigation into the murders of the two kidnapped Royal Engineers, whose bodies had been found buried outside Az Zubayr. Some of the RMPs were adamant that, although they knew who was responsible, they had been ordered to make no arrests for the time being. The suspects were prominent community leaders in Az Zubayr and there were very real fears that if a move was made, it could spark serious civil unrest.

The RMP shared the building with lots of officials, including the British envoy to Basra and some well-meaning Americans working for the UN. They spoke to me of their optimism for the future, as if they were going to wave a wand and transform the country into a peaceful democracy. I was out on the streets and knew better. Unfortunately, developments in Iraq since 2003 have been even worse than I feared.

• • •

Our interpreters played a vital role in our peacekeeping work. They became part of the team and without them we wouldn't have known what was really going on. They told us how their families had suffered under Saddam. Many had lost close relatives or suffered torture. One man showed me the scars on his feet, where he'd been brutally whipped. Now their country was under foreign occupation and I felt that they were making the best out of a bad situation.

Sometimes, they stopped misunderstandings between our men and the locals from escalating. For example, a Jock might think that an arm-waving Iraqi wanted a fight, when he was just explaining that he wanted to walk up the road to buy some bread.

I had to tackle some cultural clashes between the interpreters and the Jocks. It might be over something simple, like men showing their bare arses after a shower, and in that case we built screens to resolve the situation. Other problems arose over the trickier topic of men and women. Several times, interpreters came to me complaining that soldiers had made comments about the local beauties such as: 'Check the tits on that one.' I had a word with the Jocks. 'When in Rome, do as the Romans do,' I told them. 'We've got to respect their sensitivities.' Then I got the interpreters together and talked about the Jocks' earthy humour. 'It doesn't mean that they are going to molest your women,' I said. To highlight the fact that the misunderstanding stemmed simply from cultural differences, I pointed out, 'Some of my soldiers aren't happy when they see Iraqi men going around holding hands.' My pep talks seemed to do the trick and some of the interpreters started to mimic the Jocks on patrol, muttering comments like, 'She'd get it!' As Rabbie Burns put it: 'A man's a man for a' that.'

One night, we had a horrible introduction to a gruesome local custom.

'Contact. Gun shots. Wait. Out.' We were in the ops room. 'Contact. One female shot dead. Have arrested the suspect but a crowd has gathered. Require back-up.' We filled four Land Rovers and rushed to a piece of wasteland. Our guys were holding a plasticuffed Iraqi. As the mob howled, a young woman lay dead beside them. Her headscarf had come off and her brains showed where the bullet had fractured her skull.

The local clan chief stood out in his white robes. He shook hands with me and James. 'What is the problem?' he asked. 'This woman had committed adultery.'

'So fucking what?!' I replied. No doubt Wahlid toned this down in translation.

'This man you are holding is the woman's brother-in-law,' continued the chief. 'He was exercising his rights under sharia law. You must release him.'

'This woman was someone's daughter and probably a mother of children,' I replied. 'My men are not here to impose sharia law. They all have a mother, a daughter, a wife or a sister. That man has committed murder and he is under arrest.'

'*Laa, laa, laa,*' said the chief.

'*Naam, naam, naam,*' I replied.

The Jocks were livid and thirsting for vengeance. I called the RMP to come quickly and deal with the situation before our wrath boiled over.

THIRTEEN

The Green Box

The SAS guys at Camp Stephen fitted in well with the Jocks but there was less harmony with an SBS (Special Boat Service) crew that showed up while the SAS were away. We took Christine to collect them and their commander, Mal, from the SIS building. They looked more like beasts of burden than urban fighters, laden with bergens packed so heavy that they couldn't fit inside the Warrior. We tied these to the turret, dangerously restricting its movement, as we headed a meeting with a colonel in the Royal Tank Regiment.

'Don't get out of the Warrior until I give you the word,' I told them. However, as we reached the colonel's camp, small-arms fire was rattling and Mal jumped out to run about pointlessly with his Armalite. He wore black-leather fingerless gloves, which looked odd in the 100-degree heat.

'He's a gimme,' joked Lee, using the Jocks' term for someone who's after a medal. Perhaps he is, I thought, or else he's trying single-handedly to save the regiment's face after a recent cake-and-arse mission in northern Iraq during which the SBS had had to abandon all their kit.

Back at Camp Stephen, the SBS guys lounged around and tended to talk to the Jocks as though they were children. They wanted help on an op to capture three Ba'ath Party officials. They had identified a house. We were to throw a ring of steel around it, I would blow off the front door and they would storm in with stun grenades and nab their targets. This was routine for us but I was uneasy, not having worked with these guys before, and made Mal promise me that none of his men would go on the roof, because if we saw people up there, we would consider them to be enemy and engage them.

Before we set off, I noticed an SBS guy carrying out three of my wooden chairs.

'What are you doing with them?' I asked.

'I'm taking them to tie the prisoners to and carry them out on them.'

'No you're not. Put them back.'

'We need them,' he insisted.

Mal walked by. 'What's going on?'

'Get this arsehole to put my chairs back before I make him eat them,' I said. 'They're my best chairs, he didn't ask for them and anyway they're no use for tying up prisoners. They've not got any fucking arms and they'll break. If he'd asked, I'd have given him the plastic ones we normally use on these ops.'

Mal put the numpty in his place.

'Any more stunts like that,' I told him, 'and you can all go and sleep in the desert.'

The op went ahead that night. We surrounded the house with Warriors and I blasted the front door with the Rarden cannon. This was standard procedure, though I couldn't see how it tallied with the rules of engagement, as anyone behind the door would be obliterated without warning. The SBS crashed in through the back and we listened on the radio to stun grenades banging and then lots of screaming and crying. Mal's men came out the front door dragging some women and children. There was no sign of the three male targets.

'Two men on the roof,' Sergeant Stuart Gray of the mortar platoon radioed me. 'Is that Ali Baba? Shall we engage them?'

'Stop, stop, stop!' I shouted.

I could see two guys prowling on top of the house, dressed in black. These weren't Iraqis.

'Have you got anyone on the roof?' I asked Mal.

'No,' he said.

'Are you certain? We are about to shoot two men up there.'

A brief silence, followed by Mal's voice, now thick with panic. 'Do not fire! Those are my guys.'

James went to speak to him. 'Release the women and children,' he said. 'That's not the way we do things.'

We had acted on crap intelligence and narrowly avoided a blue on blue.

We were delighted when JP and his SAS crew returned to Camp Stephen. JP was a very mature, calm individual. One of his men was a Brummie and together we reminisced about our wild youths in the Midlands, while he wound me up with his tales of exclusive piss-ups at Basra palace. The SAS went everywhere in smart Western civvies, wearing hill-walking trousers and boots, and they drove around in top-of-the-range 4x4s. Not conspicuous at all.

In mid-April, JP asked our heads of shed to attend an important briefing and we were joined by an MI6 desk officer. He was a slight, bespectacled guy. I got the impression that he was trying to copy the SAS 'look', although, with his weedy frame, he failed to fill out his clothes.

'We have significant information about the location of weapons of mass destruction. We believe that some are buried in bunkers beneath this steel factory,' said the spy, pointing to a map.

We already knew that place, I realised. It was on the other side of al-Hayaniyah, on the road to Bridge 4 and just outside our area of operation. We had gone there when we'd sussed that this was where all the steel rods were coming from. We had been stunned by the scene. It was a gargantuan factory, about half a mile long and a quarter of a mile wide. Looters had smashed gaping holes in the walls, giving access to streams of lorries and carts pulled by donkeys, driven wildly like chariots in *Ben Hur*. A group of Irish Guards were idling at the main entrance.

'What the fuck's going on here?' I asked.

'It's an Ali Baba theme park but we're not allowed to do anything.'

'Then why are you here?'

It wouldn't happen in our gaff.

The MI6 man was talking about a green box. Apparently it held secrets about the WMDs. We were to keep our eyes and ears open and make every possible effort to find it.

We looked at each other.

'Do we know what's in this green box?' someone asked.

'I can't tell you any more about it,' he replied. 'It's classified information.'

The Jock on the front gate is more on the ball than you lot, I thought. We had made lots of local contacts and we knew the score: the real problems were murder, rape, looting and Iran – not nuclear warheads.

JP explained that we had to take control of the steel factory. 'You must stop the looting and lock the place down,' he said. 'Then the engineers will come and search for the bunkers.' I was sceptical about the WMDs but felt complimented that we'd been selected for the mission. At least it would be good for the country to stop the thieving; the steel could be used to rebuild the roads and bridges that we'd bombed.

We decided to take the Ali Babas by surprise and deploy the whole company in the dead of night. We left the recce platoon a kilometre behind us as a reserve force and sped into the factory with a dozen Land Rovers. We passed three times as many donkey-drawn carts on their way out. Their drivers didn't so much as give us a second look.

Then we got a grip when our Warriors and other heavy metal rolled in, blocking all the exits. Inside the factory, people were operating cranes to lift bundles of steel rods onto articulated lorries. The trucks looked new and had probably been nicked from Kuwait or Jordan. The stolen steel was fetching good prices in Baghdad and Iran. It was an astonishingly well-organised business.

Our interpreters used loudhailers to make an announcement: 'You are all under arrest and your vehicles will be confiscated.' The looters looked stunned. For weeks, they had been robbing the place with impunity. Sporadic shots rang out but we didn't reply. Most of the looters resisted arrest and fists, boots and sticks were swung before we had more than 100 of them in plasticuffs. I allocated a huge open-top truck with high sides for the prisoners. I hurried back to it when I heard screaming. Many of the Jocks had been cut and bruised in the struggle and now some were getting revenge, lifting the Iraqis onto the truck by their balls or their hair. I put a stop to this.

Donkeys charged off in a braying din as we cut them loose with a smack on the arse. In the crazy weeks ahead, I sometimes caught the Jocks having chariot races with captured steeds.

That night, we sent hunting parties to catch a few of the hundreds of Iraqis still hiding in the factory. We also took 15 confiscated trucks back to camp. It was surreal: I had come to fight a war and now I was driving a truck full of steel. We kept the vehicles in our car park, from where they would be taken to Camp Breadbasket. After a couple of hours, we released all the prisoners. 'Next time, you'll go to Umm Qasr jail,' I told them. 'You've got five minutes to get out of sight or we'll rearrest you.' I watched them scarper up the road.

In the morning, we surveyed the vast factory, an ocean of valuable metal spread out before us. Engineers came to look for hidden entrances and we opened a guardroom in a little building at the entrance. We still had to police al-Hayaniyah so we set up a rota of call signs to cover the factory. As we reduced our presence, the Iraqis began to pour back in. Our instructions were not to shoot unless we were shot at but we didn't have enough riot gear or men to do the job decisively. Night after night, armed with pick elfs (pickaxe handles), we fought the Iraqis in running battles, like rival football fans.

One night, as Lee drove me down a long steel-lined aisle, we spotted a group of looters, who ran off. As we reached the slowest, I jumped on his back while Lee chased the others. I dragged the man to the ground but he fought back ferociously and then two of his mates appeared. Soon I knew I was fighting for my life. I had never felt so scared. At one point, the big guy was behind me with his hands inside my mouth while his mates swung lumps of metal at me. Somehow, I shook him off and whacked him around the head with a steel rod. His ear burst open and he fell squealing to the ground. At last, I managed to pull my pistol from my vest and shot one of the other guys in the leg. His friend dragged him away, trailing blood. Aching but glad to be alive, I plasticuffed my captive and kept a foot on his neck until Lee got back.

The Iraqis had an effective 'dicking' system, using flashing lights to warn each other as we approached. These guys had years of experience surviving under Saddam. His regime had punished thieves with amputation or execution. James and I decided to go undercover. We put on shemaghs and dishdashes that concealed chest rigs with weapons. A REME guy fired up a battered old confiscated car for us. We managed to drive into the factory unnoticed and pulled up beside a bustling group with half a dozen trucks. I radioed the recce platoon and we jumped dramatically out of the car, pulling off our shemaghs. It was like *Beadle's About*, except that we got shot at and had to beat a retreat. The recce platoon arrived and located the weapon but not the gunman.

Another time, when Lee and I took a Land Rover to recce an adjacent factory, we bumped into a couple of men, one fat and one thin, loading steel girders onto a small truck. One of them fired a rifle and we swiftly reversed around a corner. Then we chased them at high speed into al-Hayaniyah.

'It's fucking Laurel and Hardy,' I said. But these comedians were trying to kill us. While Stan drove, Ollie was shooting at us through a broken window in the back of their cabin. I climbed into the back of our vehicle and stood up, firing back. As they sped around a corner, a girder fell off and the road sparkled. Then we ran into some traffic, I stopped firing and we lost sight of them. We turned another corner and spotted Ollie, now on foot. I jumped on him, cuffed him and stuck him in the back of the wagon. But where were Stan and the rifle?

We prowled up the road, pausing at each junction to look down the next street. One, two, three, four, five ... there he was, a hundred metres ahead of us, leaning on his truck and chatting to a mate! As we swung left, he flung up his arms in shock and jumped back into his vehicle. I was shooting at his tyres and, as we approached a street market, he crashed into a stall, to the traders' consternation. Then he legged it and I chased after him, wielding my pick elf. 'Keep an eye on Fatty,' I told Lee.

I caught up with Stan, who was still armed. I whacked him between the legs with the pick elf and a patch of his white trousers turned crimson. He spun around and I smacked him across the head. Meanwhile, Lee sat at the wheel, enjoying the show and oblivious to Ollie's disappearance into the crowd.

At the end of May, we were taken off steel-factory duties. Local clansmen had complained that we were too savage and Delta Company got the job. I was annoyed to learn that their commander had told his men not to use our 'bully-boy tactics'. We had carried out our orders as best we could with limited resources. Three days later, we were sent back in. Delta Company had lost control.

We were back in the middle of the farce even though the engineers had searched for bunkers and found nothing. At Camp Stephen, I caught some of my men taking the piss out of our spy.

'Hey, Speccy,' a Jock muttered within his earshot, 'have you found your green box yet? Has it got a red button?'

'Look, you fuckers,' I told them, keeping a straight face, 'I'll have you outside digging sandpits all day.'

FOURTEEN

Natural Causes

Zero tolerance meant taking lots of prisoners. As company sergeant major, I assumed responsibility for dealing with our POWs. In the run-up to the war, in Germany, I had attended a presentation on how to deal with prisoners. We had been warned to be wary of the Red Cross, as they might 'try to poke their noses in where they're not wanted' and were told that POWs should be 'conditioned'. This meant using shock tactics to disorientate them and soften them up for interrogation, including hooding prisoners with sandbags, running them through screaming gauntlets and making them adopt stress positions (such as kneeling with their hands behind their heads or stretching out against a wall) for long periods. I now know that such practices were banned in 1972 by then prime minister Ted Heath. But, despite the denials of the present government and the Ministry of Defence, this is exactly what we were told to do in 2003. My only other POW training had been on the platoon-sergeant and section-commander battle courses at Brecon in the 1990s. There, we were instructed to deal robustly with prisoners on the battlefield, hooding them, making them lie face down with bayonets at their necks and jumping on their backs with both knees.

When we established Camp Stephen, I allocated an area of about 20 sq ft for our POW cage, a canvas tent draped with camouflage net. There was one entrance, where we placed armed guards, and inside there were some jerrycans of water and a stretcher. Prisoners were to sit facing into the canvas and were forbidden to speak to one another.

Our challenge was to deal with lots of different types of prisoner. Some were prisoners of war who continued to pose a direct threat to our forces. Others were criminals, and these ranged from opportunistic looters to cold-blooded killers. As a rule, we hooded all the POWs and other dangerous prisoners on arrest and removed the hoods when they were put in the cage. The rest were usually just plasticuffed. Whenever possible, prisoners were examined by a medic. Sometimes – especially after operations at the steel factory – we were overwhelmed with prisoners. We had had no specific guidance on what to do with these less dangerous prisoners, so I usually let most of them go with a warning after a couple of hours. More serious suspects got passed up the chain for interrogation. Some went on to the main British Army prison at Umm Qasr, when it wasn't too full.

• • •

While most of our prisoners were just petty thieves, we did encounter some very serious criminal activity in Basra. At the beginning of May, we became aware that a gang of murdering paedophiles was on the loose in al-Hayaniyah. Rachel contacted James with information about a man and his two sons who, at the time of the invasion, had been awaiting execution for raping and murdering young girls. They had dumped the bodies in the Shatt al-Arab. When the regime collapsed, these men took their chance to escape from Abu Ghraib prison, near Baghdad, and head home. Now, children were going missing again.

Rachel took an informer to identify the suspects' home and, at 5 a.m. on 8 May, we sent in a raid party, led by Tam Salter of the mortar platoon. They arrested the father but found no sign of the sons. In a basement, they discovered shackles designed to fit tiny wrists and ankles and a metal bar with a lump like a golf ball welded to it. When Tam brought back these tools of torture, a wave of revulsion swept the camp.

When we removed the sandbag from his head, our captive seemed unfazed. He was a sturdy man in his late 40s. Stripped to his underwear for a medical examination, he displayed tattoos everywhere from his neck down. It was as if a child had scribbled Arabic letters, arrows and dots all over him. He got dressed and was taken to the cage.

'What is your name?' I asked him through an interpreter, who stood behind him, out of his sight. 'What is your date of birth? What do you know about the kidnappings of young children in your area?'

Instead of answering me, the prisoner became agitated, babbling about his innocence. His hands were cuffed but he lunged at me and I took his feet from under him. The guards picked him up and I told him to stay standing for a while. 'Make sure he doesn't move,' I told the guards. When I came back an hour later, he had calmed down. I got his name and date of birth and allowed him to sit down.

That afternoon, a Scottish journalist visited the camp. Tam Salter and I showed him the manacles and the club. 'I came here to fight a war and now we're dealing with child killers,' I said. The journalist went around the camp to talk to Jocks in their platoon quarters. I was in the ops room when one of the POW guards rushed in, flustered and breathless. 'Sir, there's a problem in the cage. The prisoner who came in this morning is dead.'

'What the fuck?' I said. 'Go and get the medic, now!'

I found someone to cover for me in the ops room and rushed to the cage. The prisoner was lying on his back with white foam around his mouth. There were dirty marks all over his light-coloured dishdash.

'What's gone on here?' I asked the Jocks.

'He just started rolling about on the floor,' one said, 'and then he went very quiet. He must have had a fit.'

The medic checked his heart and pulse and declared the man dead. 'We can't leave the body lying here,' he said. 'We'd best take it to the morgue.'

Turning to the Jocks, I said, 'I am reporting this to the RMP. What you tell them will determine whether or not you are going to spend the next 20 years in prison. So you'd better not have done anything wrong.'

I went to tell James, who was deep into writing a report on the operation.

'Fuck me, that's drama,' he said. 'What about the guy from the press?'

The last thing we wanted was the journalist sniffing around. I sat him down for a chat while he waited for his lift back to HQ. He was facing me with his back to the main gate as a bizarre scene unfolded behind him. A stripped-down Land Rover pulled up and the driver went to check out with the sentry. In the back of the wagon, with a strap across his chest to keep him upright, sat the deceased prisoner. We were out of body-bags. The Jock returned to the vehicle and I glared at him intently. Taking advantage of my predicament, he took hold of the corpse's head and moved it like a ventriloquist's dummy: 'We're just checking out now, sir.' Very funny, I thought – if we hadn't had a serious investigation on our hands.

Two days later, a team of four officers from the SIB arrived. They were also investigating Tommo's accident. I answered all their questions but they focused less on the prisoner's death than on the fact that he had been sandbagged on arrest.

'Why was the prisoner hooded?' they asked.

'That's what we've been told to do,' I said. 'Look, I've had no formal training on any of this,' I added.

They quizzed James about the hooding and he dug out a frago (a radio order) from battalion HQ clearly authorising this practice.

On 12 May, we went with the SAS to raid a couple of houses. We were after some Fedayeen generals who might lead us to the green box. We blocked off a street and James and I took one house while the SAS stormed another. There were only women in our house. I showed them a photograph of our target and they denied that he lived there. Then I caught one of them hiding an AK-47 behind a curtain that concealed a small arsenal. 'Tell your husband to hand himself in,' I said as we took the guns away, 'or else we'll keep coming back every day.' To my surprise, he turned up at the camp gate that night.

The SAS emerged from their raid with two captives: a commander and his number two. Back at camp, I found that the commander, a small guy, had a broken nose.

'What happened?' I asked.

'He went for a weapon and got whacked with an extendable baton,' said JP. 'I'd prefer you to leave us out of your report.'

'Sorry, but no way,' I replied. 'I don't want the SIB blaming my men and anyway it happened in the line of duty.'

The prisoner was checked by the medic and taken to lie down on the stretcher in the cage.

His second in command was a tall, solid man who reminded me of Demis Roussos.

'I am a schoolteacher,' he told me.

'You're a Fedayeen general,' I replied.

'No!'

'Then who's this?' I held up a photo of him in a green uniform with eagles on his lapel. He was silent.

I left the prisoners with two guards. After a couple of hours, one of them came to see me. 'A prisoner is dead.'

I went straight away to James. 'Sir, you're not going to fucking believe this.'

The Demis Roussos lookalike was lying on his back in a very grubby-looking dishdash.

'We don't know what happened,' said the guard. 'Heard him coughing and then he just keeled over.'

'He's got a pulse!' announced the medic.

The prisoner was driven to hospital in one of our ambulances but he died there.

The SIB extended their investigation to cover this, the second death in custody in four days. They decided that both were due to natural causes. The medic who took the bodies away told me that it would be almost impossible to carry out a conclusive post-mortem because they were decomposing so quickly. I didn't envy the guys who had to undertake these investigations: the morgue was an ISO container attached to the nearest hospital and temperatures inside exceeded 100 degrees, which can't exactly have made their jobs very pleasant.

FiFTEEN

'You Leave Me No Choice'

Life at Camp Stephen was one long round of exhausting operations. Each day was like a week and each week was a complex drama.

Meanwhile, in the wake of the chain-gun incident, I felt a deep concern for Tommo. The SIB investigation was a nagging worry. They were talking to my men about the accident, but not to me. What was going on? I was told that they wanted to interview me on 26 April, at their Umm Qasr HQ. I wondered why I had to travel there when they visited our camp regularly and had people based in Basra. When they visited us from Umm Qasr, it was in an armoured convoy. To go there, I would have to commandeer the necessary heavy metal and put several of my men at unnecessary risk escorting me in two Land Rovers on a dangerous six-hour round trip. I was furious.

The most striking aspect of the British Army base at the port town of Umm Qasr was the prisoners: thousands of them, sitting in the desert sun, encircled by barbed wire. I left my men to bake and went to see the legal adviser who had been appointed to me. 'I will sit with you but I can't get involved,' he said. What are you here for then? I wondered.

We went into a dusty room and sat facing two SIB officers, a man and a woman. They switched on a tape recorder and cautioned me that I was being interviewed under the terms of the Police and Criminal Evidence Act 1984 and the Service Police Codes of Practice. Lots of questions followed. Was I the gunner on Zero Bravo? What training did I have? How did the chain gun work? What had happened on the night of 24 March?

My memories were still raw and I gave a detailed account of the mission to rescue Barry Stephen and the accident back at the Crown Jewels.

They had done some homework on the workings of the Warrior and the chain gun and they came at me from every angle, referring to a sheaf of witness statements.

'Was the chain-gun safety switch on?'

'I have already explained that I switched the ASS to safe, as ordered by my commander, after a contact at the mosque.'

'Were you standing up or sitting down when the gun fired?'

'I was standing on the gunner's seat all the time.'

'Did you fall down and fire the gun by accident?'

'No. If you have a look inside a Warrior, you'll see that it is almost impossible to fall down from a standing position, with all your gear on, so that your foot presses down on the firing switch. And the armed selector switch is a toggle switch that you have to pull upwards.'

'Could something have fallen onto the foot firing switch?'

'I don't know.'

'Did you see anything?'

'No. I jumped out as soon as I realised something was wrong.'

'REME reports finding no fault with the gun. This has been confirmed by MSG.'

'MSG didn't come to do a proper examination of the Warrior and the gun. The REME found a positive earth fault on the Warrior.'

'The gun has never fired by itself before, has it?'

'Not in my experience but I've had lots of problems with Zero Bravo and the chain gun, and with other Warriors.'

I went through it all: the breakdowns, even as we were about to invade Iraq; the countless chain-gun stoppages, sometimes when we were embattled and fighting for our lives; the electric shocks; the time a Warrior door closed by itself and almost amputated my commander's leg.

'I don't know what caused the gun to fire,' I said, 'but I do know that I didn't do anything to cause it. I have no confidence in the chain-gun weapon system or the Warrior. There are far too many problems and they need investigating.'

My interrogators told me that they would make some more enquiries and might want to see me again.

'How do you think that went?' I asked my adviser.

'Well, it was your first statement. They might want to see you again.'

I felt extremely vulnerable. Perhaps they had brought me all the way here to intimidate me, hoping that I would admit to something? But I clung to the belief that, in the end, I would be treated fairly. This was, after all, the British Army – the institution that I had committed my life to and whose values I cherished.

• • •

At Camp Stephen, it was becoming clear that our interpreters were putting themselves at risk. 'Where's Muhammad?' I asked the interpreter we called 'Jock' one day. I hadn't seen him for a couple of days and he was usually very reliable.

'He's sick,' Jock told me.

The interpreters were all, in my experience, exceptionally honest, so I let it go at that for the time being. The next day, however, when Muhammad still hadn't appeared, I collared Jock about his absent friend. 'Just tell me if he doesn't want to work for us any more. I won't fall out with him.'

Jock chewed his lip and looked at me. 'He has a big problem with Ali Baba,' he said. 'They have threatened to kill him.'

Muhammad worked for Jimmy Russell of the anti-tank platoon. Jimmy gave me some background. They had raided a house several days before and confiscated four handguns and $10,000 that the occupants couldn't account for. Jimmy had given them a receipt for the cash, which was now being investigated by the RMP. The men of the house were detained for a while and then released. As usual, we didn't know what else to do with them. 'Muhammad knew those people but he still wanted to come on the raid,' said Jimmy. 'He said they were Ali Babas.'

I went to speak to James. 'We have to do something about this, sir,' I said. 'If we don't, it will happen to another interpreter and then another. These people have been loyal to us and deserve our support. And if we don't help them, it could cost us.'

The pair of us drove to Muhammad's home in al-Hayaniyah. It was a typical lower-middle-class set-up: a flat-roofed detached house surrounded by a high wall with a big iron gate. Muhammad lived there with about a dozen of his extended family. The man looked ill. He ushered us into a pristine living room and told us the whole story. They hadn't in fact threatened his life but they had kidnapped his ten-year-old daughter. 'They are demanding the return of the money and the guns,' he told us.

'You know we can't do that,' I said. 'But we will do whatever it takes to get your daughter back.'

'No, please do not get involved,' said Muhammad anxiously. 'The clan elder had agreed to mediate and he has summoned the head of that family.'

We made a detour on the way back, stopping at the kidnappers' house. Like me, James was eager to storm in. I thought of my own little girl. There was nothing on God's earth I wouldn't do to protect her. But we had to wait.

The next day, we learned that the clan leader had ruled against Muhammad. If he wanted his daughter back, he must get the money and the guns returned.

Muhammad came to the camp and we met in my office. 'Please, Sergeant Major. I am begging you to give them back the guns.' If I gave in, every one of our interpreters would become more vulnerable and so would we. What if they were forced to give information about our movements or even carry a bomb into the camp?

It was interesting that the gangsters seemed keener to get their guns back than their money. Our seizures and amnesties were creating a shortage, at least for the moment. Before we invaded, you could pick up a deadly AK-47 on a market stall for just $100.

Muhammad was on his knees. 'Please leave it with me,' I told him. 'I have a daughter of a similar age and I understand how you feel. Call me as soon as you hear anything.'

That evening I mounted an op, without telling James. I gathered some men from the recce platoon in two Warriors and went to the kidnappers' house. With our Rarden cannons pointing at the front door, I strode up and booted my way into the house, followed by a couple of Jocks and an interpreter wearing a balaclava. We charged in, yelling and with our rifles ready, searched the premises and herded the occupants – a middle-aged man and his three sons in their late teens and twenties – into a single room.

I handed the father a phone and looked at my watch. 'Make a call,' I told him through the interpreter. 'You have exactly one hour to ensure that that child is returned to her family. Otherwise, you and your sons are coming with me.'

The man spoke to someone on the phone.

'What's he saying?' I asked the interpreter.

'Well, he's asking how the girl is and saying that they might have to give her back.'

I grabbed the man by his dishdash and dragged him outside, telling the interpreter to follow me. We had words. I made it plain to the kidnapper that his time was running out. A puddle of urine formed at his feet. Then I told him that he could have his money back when the girl was released. We were keeping the guns but the RMP had decided that they couldn't link the cash to any crime. I'd heard this just before we'd set off and had held on to this bargaining chip.

We went back inside and the man made another call. Twenty minutes later, Muhammad called me to say his girl was home safe.

When he returned to work, Muhammad embraced me even more warmly than usual and kept offering to make me cups of tea. The kidnapper got the cash back and I made a point of going to his house again and shaking his hand. The matter was resolved but it was clear that the threat to our interpreters was growing.

• • •

In late May, the UN lifted its sanctions against Iraq and the evening skies filled with celebratory gunfire. I was in my office writing a report when the air horn blasted: under the cover of the jollity, we were being attacked. Judging by the brief time between each crack and thump, the gunmen were quite close.

Jocks ran to their oft-rehearsed defensive positions. I grabbed my rifle, body armour and assault vest and rushed to the vehicle park. We took a couple of Land Rovers and drove to a small village on the other side of the river behind the camp. Several of us dismounted. It was dark and the air was thick with the crackle of bullets.

'Gunman!' shouted Jules MacIlhenney as I turned into an alleyway. I saw the shadow of an AK-47 and caught its owner in the leg with a round from my SA80. He ran down the alley and I got up from a kneeling position and chased after him.

'Contact. Gunman. Wait. Out,' I shouted down the radio, worried that one of my men might shoot me by mistake.

The gunman ran into a shop and I followed him, thinking he'd go out the back door. As I came through the entrance, the dust on the ground danced with bullet strikes. The gunman was ambushing me from behind a fridge-freezer. He must have misfired through panic. I shot from the hip, putting two rounds into his chest. Then I stepped to the right and shot him in the head. He went down. I pulled a chair out of the way, smashing the glass shop counter behind me in my haste, and kicked his gun away from him. Then I dragged him out of the shop.

James appeared. 'What's wrong with him?'

'He's got a bit of a headache.'

James applied a field dressing to the man's gory head, though I was sure he must be dead.

Our men had flooded the village by now and we arrested more

gunmen. I later learned via military intelligence that my man was a Shia assassin who had that day killed a senior Ba'athist.

• • •

'Tell me what happened.'

The CO had summoned me to his office. It was early June, more than two months since the chain-gun accident. It was the first time that we had discussed the matter. We spoke briefly and he handed me a copy of the SIB report, as thick as a telephone directory. I returned to Camp Stephen and flicked through the many statements. Tommo's seized my attention. Signed from his hospital bed in England, it talked about how he'd guided my Warrior moments before it shot him.

He said that he didn't know what my position was but he would like to think that I had been in the turret watching him guiding us and checking that Lee was following him correctly. That was exactly what I had been doing, watching his cylume light, although he couldn't see me in the darkness.

Tommo went on to describe what happened when Christine followed him into the berm. He said that, as the vehicle lurched forward, he saw a number of flashes coming from the front of it and that right away he felt a throbbing sensation in his finger, although at that stage he felt no pain. Then he looked down and saw the bullet holes in his legs. At that moment, he fell to the ground. His statement explained that he had received bullet wounds to his right thigh, left knee and right ring finger. As a result of his injuries his left leg had been amputated above the knee. A metal pin had been used in the reconstruction of his finger, which would consequently have less mobility.

His final comments were devastating. He said that he had been asked to express his feelings towards me. At first, after the accident and the loss of his leg, he had been angry. Over time, he said, his anger had lessened although he did not feel he would be able to speak to me or face me. He said that, although he was fairly philosophical, he was saddened that his injuries would have an effect on the interaction he would have with his son, then 22 months old. In conclusion, Tommo stated that he hoped that the investigation would lead to my prosecution. He said that he would be angry if I was not found guilty or if the punishment I received was not proportionate with the degree of neglect I had shown.

I fully sympathised with Tommo but it hurt me deeply to read that he held me responsible for potentially damaging his relationship with his son. I was innocent. Had the RMP encouraged him to make such a damning statement? I spent the night licking my wounds.

The next day, I went to see Rachel and Frank Mason, who was perhaps the British Army's top expert on the Warrior and the chain gun. We met in his room at B Company HQ. 'I can't believe they'll prosecute you,' he said. 'We all know that the chain gun's a disaster waiting to happen.'

Rachel read the statements carefully. 'Look,' she said. 'The SIB people are saying that they don't want to interview you again and they are leaving the matter to your CO's discretion.'

'So my fate depends on that report.'

'Yes. But look at all these supportive witness statements. James says that you switched the gun off before you got back to the Crown Jewels. Several people, including your driver, saw you standing up in the Warrior before and immediately after the gun went off.'

She told me that if I was charged, I should opt for a court martial rather than for summary dealing. Summary dealing would mean that the brigadier would decide if I was innocent or guilty after a brief hearing, while in a court martial the witnesses would be cross-examined and the evidence considered more carefully.

'But it could be a year before a court martial,' I replied. 'I'd have it hanging over my head all that time. Even if I'm sent for summary dealing, I can't believe that the brigadier will find me guilty.'

On 10 June, I was summoned to see the CO again. Unusually, his adjutant wasn't in the room to take notes.

'What happened?' he asked me once more. 'Something must have happened. You must have slipped.'

Once more I told him that, while I knew what *hadn't* happened,

I didn't know what *had*. 'The evidence says that I was standing up and therefore could not have fired the gun,' I pointed out.

'Something must have happened,' he repeated. 'If you accept the charge of negligent discharge of the weapon, it won't affect your future career.'

In my last report, he had given me the top grade and recommended me for promotion to regimental sergeant major. But I knew I had to refuse this offer. 'You and I both know there are always problems with the chain gun,' I said. 'The weapon system needs investigating, not me. If I accept this charge and get promoted, how will I feel in a year's time if there's another accident and someone gets shot dead?'

This was a message the CO didn't seem to want to hear. 'I'm telling you that it will not affect your career,' he reiterated.

I doubted it. No matter what, it would leave me with a criminal record and a dark stain on my file. But, more importantly, I could not in good conscience 'take it on the chin' when there was a risk that the same thing could happen again.

The CO's next words stunned me. 'You leave me no choice. You will be transferred from the regiment with immediate effect to England, where you will become regimental quartermaster sergeant at 3 Divisional Signals Regiment in Bulford. Before you go, you will appear before the brigade commander on 14 June for summary dealing on a charge of negligent discharge.'

Outside, my eyes filled with tears. I felt so frustrated. If I had done something wrong, I would have held my hands up. But I was being transferred out of the Black Watch before I'd even been tried, never mind found guilty. After two decades' loyal service, I had been expelled from the regiment, effectively because I had refused to support a lie, refused to admit to doing something I hadn't done. The dreams of my youth were smashed. I was finished with the Black Watch for ever.

Davey Bruce found me in a state of shock. He was usually involved in all regimental disciplinary matters but had not been present this time. 'How can my transfer to another post in another regiment have been arranged? These things usually take months to sort out,' I raged. 'How can this happen before I've even gone on trial? What happens if I'm found innocent?'

Davey told me to focus on preparing for my hearing in four days' time. 'You'll need an accused's adviser,' he said. I went to see Colin Gray, the regimental quartermaster. As my first sergeant in the Black Watch, he had known me man and boy. Colin immediately agreed to support me. This was comradeship at its deepest.

I called Rachel. We shared an apartment in Germany but I was being sent to England and Rachel's job meant that she couldn't follow me. Our relationship as well as my career could be jeopardised. She knew this but concentrated on helping me with my trial. 'You need to make a list of friendly witnesses to call,' she said, 'and I'll ask around about the legality of your being posted out of the regiment.'

Rachel made some enquiries. In no way was she interfering in the process – she could hardly nobble the brigadier. She was just trying to get some information about my rights in an unusual situation. Nonetheless, her CO quickly contacted mine, and his adjutant called me with more bad news. 'The RMP CO is not happy that you are discussing a current case with one of his officers,' he said. 'It could be compromising. Both COs have decided that you are banned from seeing each other or speaking to each other until after the summary dealing.'

SIXTEEN

Beyond Reasonable Doubt

'Elvis', one of the local youths employed to do our washing and cleaning, had scrubbed my clothes well but he still hadn't managed to remove all the bloodstains in time for my hearing on 14 June. It was to be held at Saddam's old presidential palace in Basra. I set off in a Land Rover, my crew following on with Christine as evidence.

It was my first and only visit to the citadel that had become the British Army's HQ in southern Iraq. Its gates were about the size of Buckingham Palace's but made of solid metal. Behind them stretched a road set in lush grounds dotted with houses. Checkpoints punctuated our route to the river that encircled the palace. We parked on the near bank, close to a block of tightly guarded shipping containers filled with captured dollars – millions of them. Colin and I walked across a bridge that swept over the river to an imposing entrance of wood and brass. A soldier was fishing on the bank. Inside, everything was on a grand scale. Men were carrying double-thickness mattresses up a spiral staircase. After the squalid chaos of al-Hayaniyah, this place seemed like a wonderland.

We went to the admin area, where a platoon of laptops was set up, and waited for Major Spence, the brigadier's SO2 for discipline.

'This man's a complete penis,' muttered Colin as the major approached.

'Sergeant Major,' he addressed me, in a discordant clash of Geordie and adopted posh. 'I'd like to have a word with you in private.'

'I am the accused's adviser,' insisted Colin. 'Whatever you've got to say, I want to hear it.'

The three of us went into a room and the major put his case. 'Look, I've commissioned through the ranks and I've been in trouble once or twice myself,' he said. 'You have a great future ahead of you and shouldn't waste it. You can change your mind now and accept this charge. It will have no impact on your career.'

Colin looked at me in astonishment. I suspect he hadn't fully believed my account of my meeting with the CO. But now we were hearing exactly the same thing from the man who was advising the brigadier. It was as if they simply assumed I was guilty. Either that, or the message was: 'Shut up about the faulty weapon system, take the rap and everything will be all right.'

'If I had done anything wrong I would plead guilty,' I said, 'but I am completely innocent of this charge.'

Colin waded in: 'We're wasting time here. Let's get all the facts in front of the brigadier.'

We went back into the main hall. Several of my witnesses – James, Frank Mason and my Warrior crew – had arrived and they were ushered into a waiting room. Then Colin and I were called to the brigadier's office. It was a large room with a lofty, ornate ceiling, walls of paintings in gold frames and a door leading to an en-suite bathroom. The brigadier sat with Major Elocution behind a mammoth desk and we faced them from behind a smaller one.

Although I was still hopeful of vindication, I felt uneasy that Brigadier Brimms, the brigade commander who had led us into Iraq, had been promoted and replaced by Brigadier Bradshaw. Unlike Brimms, the new guy was a tank commander with no background in Warriors. He was a tall, slim man with tight, curly, greying hair, quite long at the back. He had piercing eyes that drilled into your face when he spoke to you.

'Are you 24683084 Warrant Officer Thomas Henderson?' the brigadier began.

'Yes, sir.'

'You are charged with conduct to the prejudice of good order and military discipline, contrary to Section 69 of the Army Act 1955, in that by your negligent handling of an L94A1 7.62 chain gun you discharged a number of rounds, thereby occasioning personal injury to 24755662 Sergeant Albert Thomson. You have the option to elect for trial by court martial or else that I deal with it.'

'I would like you to deal with it, sir.'

Although Rachel had advised me to opt for a court martial, I'd decided not to. I felt my case was strong and I had faith in the system. I also hoped for a quick resolution; a court martial could take months, maybe years. I wanted to return from Iraq with honour.

'Very well. I have looked at the facts of the case and I have the option to refer the case for court martial or to deal with it myself. I have decided to deal with it myself. Do you accept the charge?'

'No, sir.' I put my case briefly to the brigadier, drawing his attention to the supportive witness statements. It was the same message I had delivered to the SIB team: the chain gun should be on trial, not me. Then I started calling my witnesses.

Lee and others testified that I had been standing up while Tommo had been guiding the Warrior and after the chain gun had fired. From the REME, Corporals Frost and Shoemaker spoke of their brief examination of Christine in the darkness. Shoemaker had found no fault on the gun but Frost had discovered a positive earth electrical fault on the Warrior. Sergeant Curtis recalled how his crew had improvised to fix a fault in the hours before we invaded Iraq. I thought all their evidence was helpful, though I didn't have the legal training to question them forensically.

James came in and gave a crisp performance. 'I checked the turret almost immediately after Sergeant Thomson was shot and the armed selector switch was at safe,' he explained.

'Are you absolutely sure about this?' the brigadier quizzed him.

'Absolutely sure, sir,' he replied.

Frank Mason spoke at length about the many problems he had encountered with the Warrior and the chain gun.

'Have you ever known the chain gun to fire by itself?' asked the brigadier.

'No, sir,' said Frank, 'but in my opinion the weapon has not been fully tried and tested and it is a danger.'

At this point Major Elocution whispered in the brigadier's ear and he told us to adjourn for five minutes.

'They're not supposed to have breaks like this,' said Colin as we waited outside. 'But I think it's in the bag. The brigadier can only find you guilty if it's beyond reasonable doubt and there hasn't been one hostile witness.'

When we reconvened, we walked out of the palace and across the bridge to examine Christine. The brigadier climbed in via the back door and, comically, he tried to crawl up and join me in the turret, before sitting down in the signaller's seat as if that had been his intention all along.

'Would you like to climb in here, sir, and see all the controls?' I asked.

'I know what I'm doing in a Warrior,' he snapped.

He got out and climbed up into the turret to sit in the commander's seat. Wearing my bulky combat vest, I stood on the gunner's seat and showed how it would be impossible for me to fall down, switch on the armed selector switch and press down on the foot-firing switch.

'Thank you, I have seen enough,' said the brigadier.

We went back into the palace and the major stopped us outside the brigadier's office. 'We'll have another five-minute break,' he said. 'Please wait outside.'

Colin was fuming. 'What are they up to? You couldn't have fired the gun. It stands out like a bulldog's bollock.'

After ten minutes, the major came out again. 'Sorry for the delay but the general has arrived and the brigadier is speaking to him.'

That's wonderful, I thought, my whole future is in the balance and the brigadier keeps me waiting while he has a chinwag with his boss.

When we returned to our desk, Colin made a formal complaint: 'Sir, the rules state that you are not allowed to exclude participants from proceedings but this has happened twice today.'

'Captain Gray,' said the brigadier, 'I will seek advice from my SO2 at any time I want.'

'With respect, sir,' Colin persisted, 'if you refer to the summary-dealing paperwork in front of you, I think you'll find that the proceedings are meant to flow through without interruption or any exclusion whatsoever.'

We were sent outside once again and recalled after five minutes. 'You are absolutely right, Captain Gray, and I do apologise,' said the brigadier, 'and we shall carry on now.'

The proceedings seemed disorganised and I wondered whether this was because I'd been expected to fold at the promise of an untarnished career and plead guilty before the matter came before the brigadier.

'I have before me a statement from Colonel Adams of the Land Accident Investigation Team,' said the brigadier, before reading it out. Its final words carved themselves into my brain: 'There are no known circumstances of undemanded firing by the chain gun. I therefore believe that on this occasion the gun could not have fired undemanded.' I was stunned. I had not seen this statement in the evidence.

'I will now consider the facts of the case,' said the brigadier. As he flicked through his notes for a few minutes, I tried to slow my racing heartbeat to the pace of the clock ticking on the wall.

Then he looked up at me. 'I may be wrong but I have considered the facts of the case and, in the light of the evidence from the Land Accident Investigation Team, I find the case proven. I am therefore issuing you with a fine of 14 days' pay.'

The fine was almost irrelevant. But, knowing I now had to live with the stain of the conviction, I felt he might as well have blasted me with an anti-tank missile.

'Do you have anything to say, Sergeant Major?'

'No, sir.'

I stood up, saluted, turned right and marched out of the room. Colin followed me. He didn't say a word until we had left the building. 'I have just witnessed an innocent man being found guilty,' he said. Colin's words gave me a sliver of comfort as I left Saddam's palace with a criminal record.

It was a morose journey back to Camp Stephen, with everyone doing the thousand-yard stare. I told James the verdict. He went silent and disappeared. Then I called Rachel.

'I already know the verdict,' she said.

'Oh aye?'

It was less than 30 minutes since we had left the palace.

'My CO,' she explained through tears. 'He came to me and said, "You can make contact with your boyfriend now. And, by the way, he was found guilty, as I told you he would be."'

SEVENTEEN

Farewell to the Savages

Before we'd flown to war, as company sergeant major, I'd spoken to each man individually, checking that he had his passport and putting a hand on his shoulder to wish him well. It wounded me deeply that, because I was being transferred out of the regiment, I could not bring my men back home. I felt it went against the natural order of things.

On 17 June, three days before I left, I was summoned for my last audience with Lieutenant Colonel Riddell-Webster. Following procedure, he showed me my annual report. His glowing words surprised me. He had given me the top grade again, writing that I had acquitted myself with honour and should be considered for promotion. There was no mention of the chain-gun incident.

'I'm sorry about what happened,' he said.

I initialled the report, handed it back and left. I was reeling from the injustice of my conviction. The SIB, my CO or the brigadier should have recommended an investigation into the flawed weapon system. The supportive evidence from James and the others, and my absolute certainty that I had not fired the gun, should have carried more weight. I felt disappointed that, after 20 years' service, my word seemed to count for nothing. An investigation into the Warrior and the chain gun might have aggravated the army and it might not have benefited the Government, which was already getting bad press about substandard equipment, but it would have been the right course of action.

The moment I left the palace, I decided to appeal the verdict. I had to give notice of this within 14 days and quickly completed the paperwork, giving it to one of the Jocks to put in the adjutant's mailbox at the regimental HQ.

The next day I called HQ. 'You've got my notice of appeal?' I asked the adjutant.

'No,' he said.

I checked with the Jock, who swore that he had delivered it.

By this stage, I was feeling numb and just wanted to slip away quietly. But the Jocks decided otherwise and I gave in to their plan for a little send-off party. Atholl Stewart sent some men from B Company to do guard duty while we sipped orange juice and listened to a local Beatles tribute band that Talib had unearthed. They murdered the songs but we enjoyed a relaxing couple of hours.

That evening I was busy in the ops room when Neil Tomlin came in. 'The officers would like to speak to you,' he said. I followed him into James's room, where James, Jules MacIlhenney and Tim Petransky awaited me – all of Charlie Company's officers. I sat down and my chair collapsed. James jumped up, insisting that I take his, while he found a box to sit on. It was a nice gesture. Some tins of olives and hors d'oeuvres were spread out on a dusty cot bed.

'Sergeant Major,' James addressed me. 'I know how you feel about no alcohol on ops but I wonder if on this occasion you might join us in a small toast of port.'

It was well known that I had a zero tolerance approach to alcohol on the camp. Guns and booze don't mix. But this was a special occasion. 'If you insist, sir,' I grinned, and James filled some tiny glasses.

'But first,' he said, 'we all want to say something to you.' I was moved by their warm and complimentary words. We had all known each other for years. It meant everything to me that the commanders of the Savages believed that I was innocent, and were saying so.

'Now I propose a toast,' said James. 'To Big Tam!' This made me chuckle. Despite our close working relationship, I had always insisted that I call James 'sir' and he call me 'Sergeant Major'. You had to set the tone from the top, I thought, and discipline was vital for an invading army.

I was touched by their kindness but I had something else on my mind. I was about to leave Iraq and Charlie Company would follow me in a couple of weeks: what would happen to our interpreters? This worried me, because they were getting lots of threats now. Our successors were to be the Queen's Lancashire Regiment, commanded by Colonel Jorge Mendonca. I had met the colonel several times and he seemed a very professional and honest soldier. When he had visited Camp Stephen, he had asked to speak to me in private and questioned me about the tactics I had employed. I felt he wanted the hard facts rather than some rose-tinted fantasy. But I was worried that the changeover would leave my interpreters vulnerable.

Wahlid asked me to arm the interpreters and I put in a request to HQ. The response was a clear no. To me, this was warped logic: we had given guns to Abu Salem, a dangerous cleric who was smuggling stolen goods to Iran, to enable him to protect himself but I couldn't do anything for the interpreters who risked their lives every day for us. The army had even cut their pay, to less than a dollar a day. The UN was paying its interpreters three times as much. It seemed to me that the message the British Army was sending to them was: 'We don't give a shit about you.' I felt responsible because I had recruited them and put them in danger. These were honourable guys.

On my last night in Basra, I went to our diminishing armoury and then met Wahlid, Talib, Jock, Hamish and Muhammad at Wahlid's home. The SAS was forwarding our captured weapons to somewhere in Africa. There was no audit trail but I still knew that I could be jailed for what I was doing. 'These are for you,' I told the interpreters, giving them 12 handguns and some boxes of ammunition. It was a mix of weaponry, including Brownings and Walther PPKs. I showed them how they worked. It was the least I could do.

Wahlid hugged me. 'We know that the British Army has treated you very badly and we are all saddened. You are a good, honest man and God sees this. We bless your family as you have blessed us by defending us with your life.' One by one, they all hugged me.

'Thank you for your hard work and loyalty,' I said to them. 'I love my country and my regiment but I have been let down and I cannot protect you any more. The situation here is getting very messy politically and you must at all costs protect yourselves and your families. We'd all better go now, before anyone notices us.'

The next morning, 20 June, while I was packing my kit, I was asked to come and speak to the men. They were all gathered in the cookhouse, a large veranda with a desert-camouflage net to protect us from the sun; my senior NCOs were standing at the back. I looked around at men I had known since they'd joined the regiment, some of whom I'd recruited. Several of them would be killed in action in 2004.

'This is the last time I will speak to you as a member of the Black Watch,' I said. 'My conviction and early departure from Iraq should not be taken by anyone as an admission of guilt. I am completely innocent of the charge, and guilty only of being in the wrong place at the wrong time. We mustn't forget that a man lies seriously injured back in England. I feel guilty for protesting my innocence when someone has almost died.

'But what happened to me is not typical of the regiment. You must all keep supporting the red hackle. Recruitment needs to be stepped up. We have achieved great things on this tour of duty. It had been a privilege for me to be with the bravest people I have ever served with.'

I pointed to my senior NCOs, Stuart Gray, Nelly Elder, Duncy Bruce, Davey Domanski and Jim Mathieson. 'Thank you,' I said, mentioning each by name, 'for your unflinching support for the way that I do business. And I'd like to say sorry. Not that I mean it! No, I am sorry for the fact that, while we have been at work, I have always put friendship to one side. But you are my true friends.'

Then I spoke about Barry Stephen, tackling a sore that had festered within the company since the night of his death. The Jocks in the mortar platoon blamed the recce platoon vehicle commanders for taking the wrong turning and leading Barry into the ambush. I told them the full story of that night, explaining how Leathley and his men had valiantly returned to the fray, trying to rescue Barry after they realised that he was missing.

'How many of you have been in shoot-outs in the past two months?' Up went a sea of hands. 'Now think carefully about this: after you have come out of an ambush, how would you feel about having to go back in with damaged equipment?' I looked directly at the men of the mortar platoon. 'That's exactly what Corporal Leathley and his men did. Don't any of you ever forget that.

'That's all from me. Keep your shit together and keep your heads down.'

As I left the gathering, some words from James pumped air into my chest. 'That is the bravest man I have ever fought with,' he said.

Back in my room, my friend Nelly Elder came with a report. 'The boss has been singing your praises, bro. Says he'd follow you anywhere into battle.' James's praise was precious to me. This was a man who had fought with the SAS. We made a seamless team: he the thinker and me the fixer, executing and enforcing his orders. We had forged an unbreakable bond as commanders who led from the front. We could have taken a back seat, concentrating more on paperwork, especially during the ops in al-Hayaniyah. But we wanted to understand what we were sending our men into. James was normally a man of few words. To this day, I am profoundly grateful that he chose to damn the verdict against me in front of the whole company.

I gave Nelly a present for each of the Jocks, organised by Talib: 200 T-shirts, all proudly emblazoned with the word 'Savages'. Then, for the last time, I left Camp Stephen.

I stopped at the regimental HQ to hand in my rifle and place a second set of signed appeal papers on the adjutant's desk. A few of us were flying back early and we formed a convoy to drive to Basra airport. On the plane, I sat beside Davey Bruce, who had silently comforted me on the night of Tommo's shooting. Now I was leaving

Basra with a false conviction. I felt that my honour, self-esteem and future had been crushed.

At 5 a.m., we landed in Hanover, where we were met by Captain Bob Reid, the families' officer, and driven to the base in Fallingbostel. Some of the wives were waiting for us with a banner and champagne. But I slipped away, driving to my apartment where Rachel, having returned the previous week, was waiting for me.

EIGHTEEN

Fighting Back

It was a bleak final visit to my office in Fallingbostel. Four months previously, I had left it ready to return to. Instead of getting back to work, I had to pack all my photos and belongings into boxes and take them to our apartment in Hohne. I arranged to fly to England, for a week initially. There was still plenty for me to sort out in Germany, like my bank account and the apartment that Rachel and I could no longer share.

On Monday, 23 June, I arrived with trepidation at the gates of 3 (UK) Division, a huge garrison at Bulford in Hampshire. Knowing how quickly news travelled on the army grapevine, I felt as if my conviction was tattooed on my forehead.

The commanding officer, Lieutenant Colonel Mike Hudson, wanted to see me. I was being promoted to regimental quartermaster sergeant, the quartermaster's right-hand man. This felt strange in the circumstances – more like a move sideways to keep me quiet. None of it was Mike Hudson's doing, however. Today, I regard him as one of the finest officers I have ever met. The son of a late-entry officer, he was more grounded than many officers, a soldiers' man with a keen interest in their accommodation, food and welfare.

'I know this has been a very quick move,' he said, making no mention of the chain-gun incident, 'but your reports are highly impressive and you are welcome here. I am keen to resolve our logistical weaknesses and I'm sure you will play your part.'

Leaving with a slightly warmer feeling, I went to see the quartermaster, Paul Widdows. He was very friendly and took me to meet Billy King, whom I was replacing as RQMS. It was the second time that I'd stepped into Billy's shoes; in 1998, I had taken over from him as colour sergeant at Sandhurst.

That evening, I drove to my brother's home in Oxford. Bob had joined the army from school but he had left after seven years and now ran his own business. I felt shredded emotionally and needed to be near my family. In the months ahead, I often made the three-hour round trip to stay at Bob's.

Billy King and I had a busy schedule, as I had to sign for all of the garrison's equipment at the end of the week, but I found time to talk to my new boss about my conviction. Paul Widdows listened without interrupting as I poured out my story. 'You know,' he said, 'it doesn't matter. I am a logistician and I've been a tank transporter so I know all about equipment problems. Your appeal will go ahead and I will fully support you, so long as you don't bring it into work. You're due a lot of leave. Why don't you take a break and sort out your personal issues? I'll handle things until you get back.'

Hugely grateful to Paul, I booked six weeks' leave and spoke to the administration officer about my appeal.

'There's no mention of it in your records,' he said.

'But I left the paperwork with the Black Watch adjutant the day I left Iraq!'

Jesus, I thought, they've sent through the information about my conviction but they're not dealing with my appeal. For the third time, I completed a form giving notice of my intention to appeal. It only just made the 14-day deadline.

Then I heard the shocking news that six British military policemen had been killed in Majar al-Kabir. I felt guilty, working in a logistical role when my expertise was needed on the battlefield. Why did the Black Watch have to send me home early? Why couldn't they let me stay to bring my men back safely?

When I returned to Germany, all the boys from Charlie Company were back. James called me. 'How are you? The guys want you to come down for a presentation.'

'Ah, no!' I protested, embarrassed at the thought of another public appearance.

'Either you come down or they're coming to you.'

A sea of smiling faces greeted me on the Fallingbostel parade square.

'How ya doin', sir?'

'Are ye skivin'?'

James gave another rare address. 'Sergeant Major, I have been asked to speak on behalf of everyone here. Thank you for your unstinting support for me as commander and thank you from all the Jocks for being Tam Henderson.'

He presented me with a bronze plaque of a Warrior on a wooden base with the inscription: 'Company Sergeant Major Tam Henderson 2001–2003. From the Savages.' It was a beautiful gift and I was moved that they'd taken the trouble to have it made so quickly.

'I'm so glad you're all back safe,' I told them. Looking around, I could attach a story to every face. We had all experienced more in our few weeks at war than most people do in a lifetime.

James came to our apartment with another present – a silver statue of a soldier kneeling on a map of Iraq. He was no longer my commander but he was a firm friend.

Rachel and I went for a long holiday on the Isle of Skye, one of my favourite places in the world. We walked in the hills, hoping that the fresh winds would soothe our souls. But our pain was too deep. Rachel's job would keep her in Germany; she was unhappy in the apartment on her own. I was angry with the whole world, increasingly bitter about my treatment, suffering recurrent nightmares and fixated on my appeal. Soon after the holiday, our relationship fell apart.

Many units returning from active service today are given a period of 'decompression', when they are taken to a holiday resort or somewhere similar and encouraged to talk about their experiences and chill out before returning to normal life. However, there was no decompression for me – or for my Jocks, who went straight from the horrors of al-Hayaniyah back to work.

In the dark weeks ahead, I drew most comfort from seeing my daughter Hannah in Belfast. She didn't care about Iraq or chain guns. She just wanted to chat to her dad.

I went back to work and pressed ahead with my appeal. The onus was on me. There was no one to guide me and little financial support. I phoned dozens of legal firms listed in *Soldier* magazine. But I kept hearing the same message: 'Sorry, we're not qualified for that kind of case.' Then I visited a local firm, where the young, ex-army solicitor was keen to help. However, his eagerness wasn't matched by experience and I felt I needed a bigger gun. Ed Jones, my former company commander, knew all about the problems with the Warrior. He made enquiries and called me back. 'Chris Hill is your man,' he said. 'He's based in Aldershot and has a good record of handling complex military cases.'

The man impressed me. He was a senior partner in his firm and had dealt with some very big cases. His questions were relevant and inspired confidence. He soon identified a gap in our team. 'You are taking on the Ministry of Defence,' he said, 'which will not admit it's in the wrong unless it has no alternative. They will certainly have expert witnesses from the supplier of the chain gun and the manufacturer of the Warrior. These giants will fight hard to defend their reputations and between them they could blind the judge with science. You're saying that you know what *didn't* happen when the gun fired but you don't know what *did* happen. That's why you need an expert witness. Someone with a strong engineering background who can examine the Warrior and the chain gun, work out how the gun could have fired by itself and explain this to the court.'

So, Chris began the search for our expert witness. He tried several people but they kept saying that my case was 'unwinnable'. I began to lose hope.

• • •

In September, while I was preparing for the appeal, Julie appeared in my office and introduced herself. She was a signaller, just back from Iraq. Her Glasgow lilt caught my attention. After she returned from leave, she was taken to hospital with a kidney infection and came back looking poorly. We gradually got to know each other. She had joined the army to escape the poverty and violence of Glasgow's East End. I was impressed that she had been in Iraq for longer than me, on operations Telic One and Telic Two. How had she coped? We went for a meal and she told me of her frightening experiences. Though she had spent several months at a base in Kabul, Iraq had been her first time in a combat zone.

On one occasion, when she was on guard duty in Kuwait before her company crossed the border, an American attack helicopter swooped down and hovered over her. The tail gunner's hand was at the ready. She panicked and started running until the wind from the helicopter's rotors blew her into the sand. Three heavily armed Yanks surrounded her and one said, 'You're lucky. We were going to shoot you but then we spotted your blonde hair.' She nearly became another blue-on-blue statistic, partly because the Americans were so gung-ho but also because she hadn't been given desert combats and was dressed in green – the same colour as the Iraqi uniform.

She told me that her scariest nights were at the Shaibah airbase when the alarm went for incoming missile attacks. She would scramble out of the truck in which she was sleeping and hide, sobbing, in a little trench she had dug behind the vehicle. After two or three weeks, she said, she stopped crying and shut down the fear. She simply didn't care any more. A lot of soldiers in Iraq, including many men, were very frightened.

As we got to know each other, I spoke to her about my conviction and she listened. Later, she told me that she had been shocked when I told her the story. At first, she said, she did wonder. Could the gun really fire by itself? Might I have slipped? However, I had told her about all the other problems with the Warrior and, as we grew closer, she realised that I was a man who would own up if I had made a mistake.

During this time, I woke up sweating in the night, suffering from nightmares in which I handed the body of one of my men back to his wife. I was very stressed and uptight as I prepared for the appeal and Julie admitted afterwards that she had been very worried for me.

• • •

Chris Hill called me. 'There's a chap in Surrey. He's got his own engineering company, Listavia International Consultants, and he's a founding member of the Expert Witnesses' Association. From what I've heard, he could be just what we need.'

I went to Chris's office in Aldershot and a small, sturdy, intelligent-looking man with white hair stood up and gripped my hand.

'Are you Tam?'

'Yes.'

'Good morning, I'm Warren Lister. I'm very pleased to meet you.'

I immediately knew that Warren was my man. Later, I learned that he always likes to meet his prospective clients face to face so that he can suss out whether they are telling the truth.

The three of us sat down and began a council of war. Chris would press the authorities to disclose information, while Warren would study the workings of the Warrior and the chain gun. This didn't prove easy.

Warren needed to see Christine, so we applied to the judge to get access to the vehicle. We went to a pre-hearing where Judge Advocate Bayliss ruled in our favour. However, when we flew to Germany, we found that my old Warrior had been gutted, with no sign of the chain gun or the engine pack. We asked for the foot-firing switch and were told by the quartermaster that his CO had rejected the request.

Back in England, Warren complained to Bayliss about what he described as a flagrant defiance of the judge advocate's orders and evidence tampering. Bayliss demanded that the Black Watch reassemble the Warrior for the appeal.

We had expected the hearing to take place in Germany but the venue was suddenly switched to Aldershot. What about Christine? We needed her there. At first, the authorities said no, it would be too expensive to bring her. They would supply another Warrior for my appeal – a newer model with a roomier turret. 'It's like the prosecution at a murder trial submitting as evidence a gun that hasn't been fired,' I said to Chris.

On 24 March 2004, the anniversary of Barry Stephen's death and Tommo's injury, Chris and I appeared again before the judge advocate at Bulford Military Court. He ruled that my old Warrior be brought to the appeal.

Then Chris Hill secured some stunning information. Contrary to LAIT's damning evidence at my trial, there were several records of undemanded firings by chain guns, including one on a Challenger 2 tank on the day we captured Basra. This evidence had not been made available to the brigadier who found me guilty.

Warren and I visited some barracks in Tidworth, Wiltshire, to look at more Warriors and Challenger 2s. 'Warren Lister has been seconded by the MoD to examine these vehicles,' I said. 'It's because of all the problems we've been having with them.'

I felt that the prosecution's shenanigans more than justified this deception. But one guy in Tidworth knew about my case and said, 'We know the score, Tam. Don't worry, we're supporting you.'

NINETEEN

Battle for the Truth

The polished oak of Aldershot military court smelled of unassailable authority. It was Monday, 14 June 2004: exactly a year to the day since my summary trial in the incongruous setting of Saddam's marble palace.

14 June 2003. The palace seemed almost miraculously peaceful after Basra. In the grounds, senior officers strolled about unarmed, while thick mattresses were carried in for their bunks. A soldier fished in a stream. I wondered how I had been allowed inside, wearing full combat gear and thick with the grime of three months' warfare.

On the morning of my appeal hearing, I was impeccably dressed in the full Highland regalia of the Black Watch, shirt-sleeve order, with kilt and fiercely polished brogues. My 20-year loyalty to the regiment was on display; my quarrel was with the authorities, not the men. It had been a long road to this hearing and I knew that I'd probably lose. How could I hope to beat the combined might of the Ministry of Defence and the arms corporations? That's what most lawyers had told me and their opinions had seemed justified when my appeal paperwork was twice lost and vital evidence dismantled.

Inside the courtroom, I was shocked to see Albert Thomson, the man I was convicted of shooting. Tommo sat in the observers' section with his wife, his crutches propped at his side. We hadn't spoken since that night in March 2003. I'd felt cut to the bone when his statement was read out at the summary dealing, saying that he wanted me to be punished. The poor guy: there was no one for him to blame but me and he hadn't yet received a penny in compensation. I turned to face him but he stared at the ground.

My next surprise was the realisation that my unit of three was outnumbered three-to-one by the army's prosecution team of lawyers and expert witnesses from the Ministry of Defence, Alvis Vickers (the manufacturer of the Warrior) and Page Aerospace (the suppliers of the chain gun). At least I had a good team. Chris Hill had had the balls to take on my case and, from our first handshake, I knew that Warren Lister had the heart of a lion. He was one of the best engineers in the country and, as an expert witness, he would tell the court the plain truth. That was all I wanted.

We stood to attention as Judge Advocate J.F.T. Bayliss and his panel of two senior officers – Lieutenant Colonel Jeffries of the Intelligence Corps and Major Rogers of the Corps of Royal Engineers – took their elevated seats. In the days to come, I would feel their eyes boring down into me. I gazed blankly ahead, keen to conceal the anxiety betrayed by my sweating hands and legs.

The case opened with our challenge to an expert witness for the prosecution. A major from the REME was put forward as a chain-gun guru but questioning by Chris Hill and the judge revealed that he was essentially an administrator with limited technical knowledge. My solicitor took the opportunity to point out, 'Sir, unlike the prosecution, I only have one expert. And mine happens to not be connected with either the manufacturer or the army.' It was a welcome little victory when the judge dismissed the witness.

After that, the judge proceeded to scrape the scab off an ugly wound by reading out my conviction: 'Conduct to the prejudice of good order and military discipline, contrary to Section 69 of the Army Act 1955, in that he, in Iraq, on the 24th day of March 2003, by his negligent handling of a L94A1 7.62 chain gun, discharged a number of rounds, thereby occasioning personal injury to 24755662 Sergeant Albert Thomson.'

Then he struck a reassuring note: 'I should say to my colleagues that this is of course a complete hearing, from the beginning, of that charge and we will start as though this is a completely fresh trial of that charge.' I was grateful for the judge's words. With his beard and greying hair beneath his legal wig, he was a considerable presence. I had met him before at pre-hearings, when he'd ruled that the army should give us full access to my old Warrior and he seemed like a fair-minded man. However, my experiences had made me wary, and to me his words were just that – only words. Throughout my career, I had always trusted my military masters implicitly but, on that day at Basra palace, that faith had been crushed. As far as I was concerned, it remained to be seen whether I would receive a fair trial.

Colonel Jones, the prosecution barrister, gave a predictably partial outline of my case. I instantly disliked this large, sweaty, spotty man who had probably spent his career pushing pens and shining his backside while I was at the military coalface. He fired verbal bullets at me, although, in the days to come, he often had to backtrack when challenged by the judge. I was amazed to hear Jones admit that the Warrior had electrical faults, although he argued that these had nothing to do with the accident. It was all down to human error – mine. I felt that the implication of his remarks was that because I wouldn't own up, we all had to sit through a complex trial. He threw in a couple more dodgy arguments, claiming that if I had been standing up in the Warrior, I would have been thrown out when it suddenly dipped into the ditch and then that if the gun had fired by itself, it would have kept on firing until someone switched it off. In the days ahead, we had to prove that he was talking rubbish.

Momentous though the trial was, I had something else on my mind as I sat in court that day. Whatever the verdict, my life was changing. Julie had called me over the weekend from France, where she was involved in the D-Day commemorations. I immediately guessed why she was crying.

'What's going to happen?' she asked.

'You'll get fat,' I replied.

• • •

The next day's session started with evidence from eyewitnesses to the accident in which Tommo was injured. My memories were still raw.

24 March 2003. We went to rescue Barry Stephen but returned with his body. Mine was the last crew back at the Crown Jewels and the other vehicles blocked our way. James went to see the commanding officer, leaving me in charge of the Warrior. I loosened my chinstrap to shout down to the men on the ground, 'Can anyone guide us through?' Tommo came forward. Following procedure, he became our ground commander and guided Lee while I stood up with my feet on the gunner's seat and my head and shoulders above the turret, watching him walking backwards. I focused through my Raven sight on the blue light of his cylume and thought about Barry and his family.

The light dropped as Tommo seemed to stumble. We halted and started moving again when he got up. Then we dipped violently into a ditch. I felt the front cone hit the earth and I was knocked back and forth against the edge of the turret, jolting my helmet and radio off my head. I heard a noise. Had we crushed him? I climbed out of the turret and jumped down as the headlights came on. He was lying, face down on the slope of the sandbank, blood seeping from the back of his left thigh. I heard shouts of 'Medic!' I was stunned. What had happened? It must have been the chain gun. Lee confirmed that he had heard it and seen the tracer fire. But how?

Then James was with me. 'That vehicle must be isolated and inspected. No one can use it,' I said. He went to check that all the switches were at safe. Tommo was stretchered away. Then the commanding officer came up. 'What have you done?'

I didn't say anything. It didn't so much as occur to me to protest my innocence. 'What do you mean?' I thought.

The Warrior was driven back to where we had been heading. I followed it and watched as an armourer and then an electrician climbed in and tried to inspect it with torches in their mouths in the pitch black. Then I spent all night sitting on an exposed sand dune, gazing down at the vehicle we called Christine. She had, I thought, just killed one of our men.

It was revelatory to hear the story from the witnesses' perspectives. Private Alan Mowbray told how, standing nearby, he had dived for cover when the chain gun fired, thinking that we were under attack. Then he'd heard Tommo screaming.

Lee Kirby explained that he had applied the brakes as the Warrior tipped into the ditch. I wasn't happy to learn what he had shouted to me when the gun fired: 'You've shot him! You've shot him!' With my radio ripped off, I hadn't heard this at the time. But Lee's immediate reaction was understandable. And – like every other eyewitness – he confirmed under cross-examination that I was standing up when the gun went off.

Jones asked, 'In what position did you see him in the turret, if you can help us, please?'

'He must have been standing up because he had a quite high profile.'

'Well, if you can't remember, Corporal Kirby, do please say.'

'No. I never said I can't remember. I said he was standing up because he had quite a high profile.'

Standing, I could not have pressed the foot-firing switch. It was a vital detail that I hoped the judge and his panel wouldn't miss. Lance Sergeant Ian Forat, a witness for the prosecution, had already confirmed that to fire the gun you had to select the chain-gun option on the ASS and then press the foot-firing switch. The position of the ASS is reflected in the colour of a light displayed on the panel: green for safe, red for the Rarden cannon and amber for the chain gun. He explained that the ASS is a toggle switch that you must pull forward and raise. I hoped the judge would realise that I couldn't have flicked it on by accident. It was pleasing that all these witnesses – though called by the prosecution – helped me simply by telling the truth.

After Lee had been cross-examined, Staff Sergeant Tim Curtis told the court how, shortly before the invasion, his team spent a night at Barnsley on the Kuwaiti border fixing an electrical fault on my Warrior. It turned out that a connector had melted in the cabling linking the power pack to the hull. They resorted to a botch job, soldering the cable and patching it with insulating tape.

Then electrician Corporal Carl Frost took the stand. He and armourer Lance Corporal Shoemaker were the men I had watched on the night of the accident inspecting the vehicle. The day before, Jones had urged the court to pay special heed to their evidence. No doubt he hoped they would just confirm that they had found no problem with the chain gun. But we were all in for a surprise. It turned out that Corporal Frost had agreed with me all along.

25 March 2003. After a sleepless night on the sand dune I had to focus. There was still a war to win and the men of my company looked to me for leadership. We were ordered to take an intelligence officer to Bridge 4. We were to take Christine. What were they thinking of? The vehicle was plainly unsafe. I spoke to James, then listened as he argued the case with Captain Clarke of the REME.

James demanded that the LAIT's mobile support group be brought up from Kuwait to do a full inspection. Clarke said it was too dangerous for them to come. Yet food and water were being delivered via a secure corridor from Kuwait. I couldn't understand why they couldn't come to investigate this dangerous vehicle.

'Are you telling me you honestly believe this vehicle is safe?' asked James.

'I am satisfied that my armourer and electrician found no fault that caused the gun to fire. It was human error,' came the reply.

But in court, 15 months later, Frost told a different story: 'I would have liked to have had it taken away and stripped. That's what I would have liked, sir. If it had gone off once because of an intermittent fault, I wasn't happy with it being in a position where it could do it again . . . The only way to check as thoroughly as I would have liked . . . was to strip the turret . . . I was told by Captain Clarke at the time it wasn't realistic.'

Frost confirmed that he had found a positive earth fault on the vehicle and that, by the time he examined it, Shoemaker had already dismantled the chain gun, inadvertently removing any evidence of electrical problems.

Chris Hill quizzed him about the implications of a catalogue of recorded problems with Warriors: 'So turrets can rotate, doors can close, lights can come on. Any reason in your mind why, in the right circumstances, the weapon system should not fire? . . . Why could not the same thing happen to the weapons as happens to the door?'

'Given the right circumstances, sir, it could.'

And this from a witness for the prosecution.

• • •

Wednesday started with evidence from Lance Corporal Shoemaker. He echoed Corporal Frost: they had both wanted the Warrior quarantined and thoroughly inspected by the LAIT's mobile support group. After the accident, he had stripped the gun to examine its mechanics, but not its electrics, which were Frost's area. He said that he didn't like the chain gun at all because it had so many stoppages.

Shoemaker outlined some fundamental flaws in the weapon system. If live rounds are fed into the chain gun when the armament armed switch is off, they will rotate and pop into an ejection tube where they can explode and cause injuries. Rather than spend money tackling this defect at source, in 1989 the army issued a standing order that the AAS was to be kept on at 'fire' at all times. So – unlike the Rarden cannon, the SA80 and other weapons – the chain gun was used without a mechanical safety catch. And there was an additional problem of rounds 'cooking off', overheating and exploding, when the gun jammed. You were meant to wait ten minutes for it to cool down – not ideal in a battle. I was pleased to see the judge taking a keen interest in these shocking facts.

In the afternoon, Lieutenant Colonel Adams of LAIT was called. He claimed that he didn't know of a single undemanded firing in his seven years of chain-gun investigations. At the summary dealing, the brigadier had cited Adams' report when he found me guilty. The gist of the argument was: 'It hasn't happened before and so it can't have happened.' But by now, a year later, we knew of several other undemanded firings.

Over a few days, the prosecution's expert witnesses were cross-examined. They had two things in common: none of them had fired a chain gun in anger and none of them was independent – they all worked for the MoD or a supplier of the chain gun or Warrior.

Glen Eggleton, a former army gunnery instructor, argued that the chain gun would never fire unless the ASS showed amber and the foot-firing switch was pressed down. But he also told the court of an incident in which a Rarden cannon had fired accidentally because of a positive earth fault. He speculated that, if I had failed to put the ASS to safe, the foot-firing switch might have been depressed by dislodged gear in the turret as the Warrior hit the ditch.

Chris Hill put it to him that, with a positive fault on the Warrior, the current could bypass the ASS and go straight to the gun: 'In your theory, the armament selector switch has to be selected to chain gun?'

'It's not in my theory, sir, that's what is in the book. That's what needs to happen.'

'What would happen if there was a short circuit beyond the armament selector switch? Would it bypass the armament selector switch completely?'

'I couldn't tell you, sir. I've never heard of that happening.'

'No. If I bypass the ignition light on my car by taking the two cables and joining them, the switch has been bypassed, has it not?'

'If you can, sir. Yes, sir.'

The expert evidence continued with a witness from the Warrior's manufacturer. There were hours of discussion and charts showing the Warrior's wiring. Despite the confusing complexity, a key fact emerged. Unlike in a car, the Warrior's electrical system is isolated from the chassis; however, if there is a positive fault, the whole hull and turret becomes live. If there is an accompanying secondary fault, things go badly wrong with the vehicle and its weaponry. But the witness said that 'to undertake a formal design analysis of double faults [would be] a mammoth undertaking' and that it was 'not usual to assess double-fault failures'.

At times, I felt like standing up and shouting, 'Can't you see? It's obvious that it was down to electrical faults!' It was an unsettling experience, listening day after day to people talk about you and the things you were alleged to have done. I imagined viewing it on a TV screen in another room, watching everyone in the courtroom watching me.

The judge then quizzed the witness about the recurrent problem of the foot-firing switch getting stuck, which could allow the gun to fire on its own as soon as the ASS was switched to amber. He described the problem as potentially 'extraordinarily dangerous'. Nothing had yet been done about this apart from issuing Warrior crews with wire brushes to keep the switch free of dirt.

'Are you able to help us?' asked the judge. 'You told us that a design change is in train for the foot-firing switch.'

'Yes.'

'Are you able to tell us when that was authorised?'

'The work on that particular task has been in motion for some time. It has had a relatively low priority status issued to it . . . The priority status of that has changed recently.'

'You have not answered my question. You have said that it was a low priority; it has been in hand for some time. Are you able to help us with for how long it has been in hand? Are you talking about a year, two years, five years?'

'Some years. Some years, sir.'

'Sorry?'

'Some years . . . I think three. Between three and four years, I believe . . . it was given a low priority initially, and therefore it really gets put to the back of the queue.'

'Yes. Is it within your knowledge as to why the priority has been increased?'

'No, sir . . . I don't work for that department.'

Next came an expert witness from the chain gun's supplier. He answered questions about the gun and conceded that, since power was being permanently supplied to the gun, it was conceivable that foreign bodies such as shards of ammunition could create a short circuit within the control unit and cause the gun to fire.

After lunch on Thursday, the court heard a summary of my

interview under caution with the SIB in Iraq. I was overwhelmed with bitter memories but pleased to be reminded that I had unswervingly asserted my innocence.

30 April 2003. Basra. We had been involved in bloody skirmishes almost daily. I was worn out. I felt I was fighting a war on two fronts as the unfair prosecution hovered over me. I was outraged when the SIB said it was too risky for them to come to Camp Stephen to see me. Instead, I had to put my men in the firing line, taking a team on a dangerous three-hour drive south to Umm Qasr. It compounded the indignity of my interrogation.

Then the court adjourned for the weekend. The past weighed heavily on the future. I had been ruthlessly expelled from the regiment I loved, yet I wished I had enough time to go with Julie to our Fife hideaway, a small cottage I had bought in the village of Culross, deep in Black Watch country, where even our milkman and window cleaner were veterans of the regiment. I wondered about Tommo. Did he think I was an evil man? Did his wife think I was evil? How were his children?

On Monday, I would fight for the truth – for Tommo's benefit as well as mine – against men I had always regarded as honourable. In preparation, I pressed my uniform and shined my brogues.

• • •

At ten o'clock on Monday morning, I stood rigid in the dock and took the oath. I had agreed with Chris Hill that we should immediately free a skeleton from the cupboard.

'I have to ask you this,' he began. 'Do you have any criminal convictions of any sort?'

'I have one conviction for fighting on my return from the Royal Military Academy Sandhurst whilst intervening in a soldier's altercation with the duty sergeant.'

It had been as simple as that: I'd jumped in to defend the sergeant and ended up thumping his assailant. It wasn't a civil criminal conviction, so I didn't have to declare it, but at least now the prosecution couldn't make ammunition of it.

Then we all went outside, where I donned my body armour, assault vest and helmet and waited for Christine to be driven into the courtyard. She had been rebuilt and looked better than when Warren and I had last seen her – in Fallingbostel, all gutted with her wires hanging out – though her paintwork was still chipped by bullets. It was a huge achievement to have Christine brought across from Germany. The prosecution had opposed this on spurious economic grounds, saying another Warrior could be brought from the nearest base. Of course, this had nothing to do with wanting to show the judge a newer model with improved internal ergonomics . . .

Memories of Christine flooded back.

March and April 2003. I'd trained in her, lived in her, fought in her, killed in her. She'd protected me, frustrated me with her frequent breakdowns and made me take the blame for her shortcomings. If only she could talk, there was so much she could say. In the days before we captured Basra, James and I took turns grabbing 40 winks inside her while the other kept watch. This was called 'emergency battle sleep' and it was highly uncomfortable in her cramped confines. One night, we unfurled our sleeping bags and slept lying beneath her arches for cover. But our comfort ended when the adjacent truck exploded, hit by a mortar, and Christine was rocked by shrapnel. Within seconds, we had scrambled back into her womb.

We spent an hour examining Christine. I climbed in and out of the turret, stood up – as I had been at the time of the accident – and sat down on my gunner's seat. The back doors were open so that everyone from the court had a clear view. Surely it was obvious that I could not have slipped into a seated position? Yet this was the only way my foot could have reached the foot-firing pedal. Wearing my body armour, it was almost impossible. At the least, I would have broken my nose, chin or teeth as I bashed against the metal rim of the turret. I was pleased to see the judge get stuck in. Even with his waterproofs – much less bulky than my gear – he had difficulty moving about.

Back in court, I took the stand and followed our plan to direct all my remarks to the judge rather than the lawyers. Chris Hill began by asking me about the highlights of my career, including my time as an instructor at Sandhurst. Then he encouraged me to recount the woeful tale of our shoddy equipment. I recalled the time my previous commander Major Ed Jones's leg had been trapped in a Warrior's electrically operated rear door.

October 2002. I knelt down, yelling to the driver as Ed wrapped his arms around me. He was screaming in agony as four tons of metal began to crush him. Fortunately, the driver cut the power before it finally slammed the door shut, and Ed's legs were saved. We reported the incident to LAIT but heard nothing back.

I told the court that it was routine for drivers to keep Warrior engines revved at much more than the officially stipulated 1,100 revs per minute to try to keep the chain gun working. I'd managed to get a faulty gun replaced in Kuwait only for the new one to jam during our sole exercise with live ammunition. Then it happened again during the battle at the barracks in Az Zubayr.

March to June 2003. The day after the chain gun injured Tommo, we came under fire at Bridge 4 and I was jolted by an electric shock as I switched on the main armament armed switch. After that, I always kept it switched off. I didn't want it to fire on civilians as we drove through the streets of Basra. Even on dangerous arrest missions with the SAS, we kept it switched off. The only exception was when I fired into the ground to halt a mob wanting to immolate the crew of a downed US Cobra helicopter. So I fought most of the war with one arm tied behind my back, unable to use my main weapon.

Jones took the floor and started to probe for weaknesses. However, my confidence blossomed as I parried his thrusts and tried to explain to the deskbound colonel the realities of desert combat. I almost choked when he suggested that chain-gun stoppages were 'normal and routine' and stoppage drills 'no great shakes'. I'd already explained that lives depended on the system and that the constant jamming was therefore a serious problem. I replied, 'I wouldn't say that having several stoppages on a weapon system which has just been put together is normal and routine.'

We talked about how my helmet and radio had been whipped off my head during the accident as we lurched into the ditch.

'And you were worried about these rather sensitive communication systems in it?'

'I think a man being shot in the leg is a bit more important than a communication system, sir.'

Jones kept wandering down what I felt were blind alleys, with irrelevant questions. The judge put him right once or twice when he forgot my answers and repeated himself. I wondered if perhaps he wanted me to snap and come across as headstrong. But I kept my cool.

Bizarrely, he quizzed me about the plates we had dropped in the ditch as we dashed away from our meal to look for Barry Stephen.

'You were not particularly amused by this debris, were you, Mr Henderson, you were a bit irritated when you saw the debris, the discarded rubbish?'

'It was me that discarded part of it, sir. I was eating as well and the reaction and speed was the reason for discarding whatever you were holding if it wasn't relevant to a battle.'

The colonel even suggested that the gun had 'performed quite well' during the battle at the barracks. I replied, 'No, it did not, sir. I had two severe stoppages and several minor stoppages. Two of them [required] field stripping. That gun let me down and nearly cost us our lives and the lives of the dismounted troops.'

After a while, the judge brought this line of questioning to an end, saying, 'Well, we know perfectly well that the gun fires; we know perfectly well that it jams. The issue in this court is whether it fires undemanded or not. I would be grateful if you could confine your cross-examination to issues which are relevant to the court.'

After four hours in the dock I stepped down, relieved that I had done my best. But would it convince the judge?

Next, my former company commander James Ord took the stand. We had lived and fought together throughout the war and had become friends. I felt sorry that his career could have been damaged because he had stood by me and told the truth at the summary hearing. His evidence had not been accepted and thus his integrity had been questioned. At the end of the war, James had been given an indifferent report – a scandal in my opinion, given his heroic performance in the line of fire. Such was the system that I had served unquestioningly for 20 years. That day in Aldershot, James spoke quietly and precisely, his arms folded across the top of the witness stand.

24 March 2003. The Crown Jewels. As we munched our boil-in-the-bag evening meals, word came that Barry Stephen was missing after an ambush on the outskirts of Az Zubayr. We'd already had bad news that day. Sergeant Roberts of the Royal Tank Regiment had been killed by his own tank in a blue-on-blue incident that might not have been fatal had he been issued with enhanced combat body armour. And two Royal Engineers had gone missing in Az Zubayr earlier on. We later learned that they had been tortured and executed.

'We're going in to get our guy out,' I said. We immediately set off, stopping briefly to rendezvous with Corporal Leathley, who had led the ambushed party. Although in shock, he got back into his armoured vehicle to lead us to where Barry was last seen. We headed to Az Zubayr, driving and firing: one vehicle laid down covering fire as another advanced and then we swapped roles. As we approached a large blue mosque, James stood up in the turret, using his night-sight to identify a shape on the ground. We directed in the other call signs, including Zero Alpha with Lieutenant Colonel Riddell-Webster. A Warrior drew up and two crew ran out to pick up Barry Stephen. Through my night-sight, he looked limp and lifeless. I felt bleak – just four days since we had crossed the border and I had lost another man from my company.

The other call signs withdrew as we told them that we would stay to take protective action. Zero Alpha was behind me. To our right we came under fire. I traversed my Warrior turret, identified weapon flashes and neutralised the enemy with the chain gun. Traversing back to my left, I saw a two-man RPG team. I was sure they were about to attack the commanding officer's vehicle and killed the man who was kneeling down with an RPG launcher on his shoulder.

Then James gave the order, 'Target destroyed. Target stop.'

*Instinctively, I switched the ASS to safe. The man standing up escaped.
'Target stop,' I said. I wasn't happy. That guy was feeding the RPG rounds
and I was ready to kill him. But it was James's call.*

In court, James laconically explained that he would never forget
ordering me to switch off the gun. It had been a matter of life or
death.

Chris asked him, 'Perhaps you could just explain your reasoning.
Why did you think it was not necessary to eliminate [the second
man]?'

'I didn't think it was absolutely required to shoot him . . . I
terminated the engagement in the usual manner, saying, "Target
destroyed."'

'And did he respond?'

'He did. He replied. "Target stop." . . . I do remember giving
that order, absolutely, because I was fairly clear that if I had not
given that order RQMS Henderson would have shot the second
man, quite rightly and understandably. It was within the target
area . . .'

' . . . The normal procedure then, of course, would be for him to
select the ASS back to safe and the green light to come on, would
it not?'

'That's correct.'

James was asked if the ASS was on safe later that night when he
checked the Warrior immediately after the accident.

'It was, yes. I don't have a mental image of those lights but that was
the purpose of my climbing up on that vehicle and I am absolutely
sure that if they were not safe then I would have taken immediate
action.'

I was comforted by what James said about my integrity: 'I wouldn't
doubt his word at all. I would believe exactly what he was telling
me.'

Chris replied, 'And if he were a man who had had a negligent
discharge, do you think that he would be someone who would front
up and admit it or someone who would lie about it?'

'I think he is someone who would admit it.'

Before Warren Lister stood to give evidence, Chris persuaded the judge to accept his written report as admissible. At first, the judge tried to rule it out and was I glad that he accepted it in the end. The report looked beyond the immediate circumstances of the accident and robustly criticised the chain-gun system. It exposed the fact that men had been sent to war with shoddy gear.

Warren exuded professional authority in court. He succinctly explained fundamental problems with the deployment of the chain gun. Originally, it had been designed to fit the undercarriage of US helicopters, where it was cooled by the engine's slipstream and the ammunition was gravity-fed. On the Warrior in Iraq, it was turned upside down in searing desert heat and the ammunition had to be powered up to it. This caused many stoppages and the lack of a safety catch made the chain gun inherently unsafe. There had been no proper examination of my Warrior and the evidence had been destroyed but, he said, it was likely that a mixture of electrical faults had caused the gun to fire as Christine had jolted to a halt nose down in the ditch.

Next came my former instructor Sergeant Major Frank Mason. Frank knew the score; he had fought in a Warrior. He told the court that I had consistently got a six in my training as a gunner, the highest score possible.

• • •

Wednesday, 23 June 2004. This was to be decision day. I felt keenly the truth of the old saying: 'It is better to die on your feet than to live on your knees.' The morning started well when Captain Colin Gray took the stand as a character witness. He had been my first sergeant in the Black Watch and had glided up the ranks to become quartermaster. I was moved by his comments. He said, 'WO2 Henderson is probably one of the most professional soldiers I have had the pleasure to serve with in all my career.'

Chris then asked him, 'Do you think it is possible, in the heat of battle, that he might have lost his head and made a mistake?'

'Once again, if he did, it would be the very first time. His character does not allow him to do that . . . professionalism is the name of his game.'

The judge quizzed Colin about the summary dealing, for which he had been my accused's adviser, and he spelled out the facts. There had been written statements only, no cross-examinations, a cursory inspection of the Warrior and no expert witnesses.

Chris made an effective closing address, getting to the heart of the technical flaws that the authorities seemed desperate to conceal. 'Interestingly, this is the only gun system in the army where this could have happened, is it not? Is that a coincidence? Any other gun system in the army has got a safety catch. This is the only gun system where it can be fired electrically. Is that a coincidence or is that a significant cause of the problem?

' . . . if it is not a technical fault, you have to consider this, I would submit. There are electric shocks coming from the hull but they are not related to the problem we have here. There are ongoing problems with the Warrior generally but they are not related to the problem we are arguing about here. There are stoppages on the gun but they are not related to the problem we have here. There are door closures but they are not related to what we are talking about. There is a pack lift at Barnsley with a botch repair made but that is not related to the problem. The shock that Henderson gets at Bridge 4 the next day is not related to this problem. These are all pure coincidences, and the jolt forward at the instant the gun fires, this is all unrelated to this case. That is the argument.

'The alternative, of course, is there is something very fundamentally wrong with the Warrior's design and they are all related and that is the cause of the problem.'

In conclusion, he cited the Military Covenant: 'It actually says in the core values of the army that soldiers volunteering for the British Army accept that by putting the needs of the service before their own, they will forgo some of the rights enjoyed by those outside the armed forces . . . but in return they can expect at all times fair treatment and to be valued and respected as an individual. Gentlemen, I do not think Mr Henderson has been treated fairly at all and I would ask you to say that that is your conclusion and to restore his reputation and to turn this conviction over.'

Judge Advocate Bayliss briefly adjourned the court before returning to give his judgment. I stilled the chatter in my brain, preparing myself for the worst. As he spoke, I looked up at the two members of his panel, trying to stay expressionless. I wanted to silently convey the message: 'Whatever you have decided, I know the truth.'

The judge spoke for half an hour, detailing the undisputed facts about the accident and Tommo's injury. He restated the legal position about negligent discharges. Is this it, I thought? He won't be able to help me? The law is the law and I am forever its victim? As he went on to review the evidence from Corporal Frost, Lance Corporal Shoemaker and James, I felt detached and these magical words scarcely registered: ' . . . we found the appellant to be a truthful witness and a highly professional soldier. We also heard evidence, which we accept, that if he had caused a negligent discharge, his integrity and professionalism would lead him to admit the fact. The evidence therefore leaves us sure that at the time the gun fired the armament selector switch was at off.'

I started to hear him again. He was saying that the cause of the firing could never be proven because the evidence was destroyed. And then this: 'From all the above, it follows that we are sure that WO Henderson did not negligently handle the chain gun and did not cause it to discharge the rounds which injured Sergeant Thomson. We therefore allow the appeal and quash both the finding of the appropriate superior authority and the fine . . . imposed by him.'

A whoop from Warren and then he and Chris were slapping me on the back. 'No,' I said, still in a daze.

I looked back over my shoulder towards Tommo. He did not respond. I stood up and walked down the aisle, pausing momentarily beside him. Nothing. I walked on and out of the courtroom.

Colin Gray embraced me. Through him, I felt the warmth of the men of the Black Watch. 'Go back and tell them about this,' I said, choked. One week later, Colin resigned from the army.

Back in the defence-team room, with Warren, Chris and my brother Bob, there was a knock on the door. I was astonished when the judge and his advisers came in to shake my hand. 'I wish you all the best,' said the judge, 'and hope this experience doesn't change your commitment to the army.'

Easier said than done, I thought. My delight at his support was tempered by disappointment. He had rightly found me innocent but I wished he had used his position to demand an independent inquiry into the real guilty party: the chain-gun system.

I went outside to call Julie and, after a quiet celebratory glass of wine, I drove back to Andover and took up my life anew.

TWENTY

Back to Hell

Before my appeal, I had learned that the MoD had rejected Tommo's claim for compensation. The man had lost a leg because of a faulty weapon system and the army wouldn't pay him a penny. I thought my vindication in court might make a difference and asked Warren to write to Tommo offering help if he opted for legal redress.

I was busy as the RQMS at 3 Division and enjoying good relationships with my colleagues, especially with my CO, Mike Hudson, who had been hugely supportive during my appeal. But most of my nights were still spent sweat-drenched and haunted.

Banished from the Black Watch, I followed the fortunes of my comrades with a mixture of anxiety and guilt. They were back in Iraq and I should have been there with them. On 12 August, Private Marc Ferns from the Black Watch was killed in Basra by a roadside bomb. He was just 21 and had taken part in the 2003 invasion. His grieving mother appeared in the media urging Tony Blair to bring the troops home. She said that she hadn't wanted her son to go back to Iraq and would 'give every penny in this world to have him here'.

The bad news continued when the Black Watch was sent to Camp Dogwood, 25 miles south-west of Baghdad. They were a 'relief in place' force, covering for US marines sent to hammer Fallujah. Charlie Company had been dissolved and the men's expertise was spread among the remaining companies. But the Savages were still in the thick of it. On 29 October, Private Kevin McHale drowned inside his Warrior when a bridge collapsed. On 4 November, three Jocks – including two more of my Savages – were killed by a suicide bomber at a vehicle checkpoint. The victims were Sergeant Stuart Gray of the mortar platoon, Private Scott McCardle of the recce platoon and Private Paul Lowe. An interpreter was also killed.

Jules MacIlhenney called me from Basra. 'Have you got a copy of The Collect?' he asked. 'The padre wants to read it at the airport when we repatriate the bodies. We don't have a copy here.' I found the regimental prayer and read it down the phone to Jules:

Oh God, whose strength setteth fast the mountains, lord of the hills to whom we lift our eyes, grant us grace that we of the Black Watch once chosen to watch the mountains of an earthly kingdom may stand fast in the faith and be strong until we come to the heavenly kingdom of him whom has bidden us watch and pray.

Then, on 8 November, Private Pita Tukutukuwaqa, a Fijian in the Black Watch, was killed by a bomb that blew his Warrior off the road. The Jocks spent a grim November at Camp Dogwood, subjected to frequent rocket attacks (an experience that would be captured in *Black Watch*, Gregory Burke's award-winning play). I felt terrible as I watched the TV news. This was the first operational tour in twenty years that I had missed. When the regiment returned to Basra, six men were dead and many more injured.

• • •

Back in January, when I'd arrived with Warren in Fallingbostel in the vain hope of examining my old Warrior Christine, the new Black Watch CO, Lieutenant Colonel James Cowan, asked to see me. It was an odd meeting. 'You are still on course to become an RSM,' he said, 'though I'm not sure if it'll be with the Black Watch.'

'I've stopped thinking about my career until after my appeal,' I told him. 'I don't want to be distracted by dangling carrots and I don't believe I'll be promoted any further.'

His predecessor had told me that a guilty plea would not affect my career but I hadn't believed this was true. To commission through the ranks, you needed an exemplary personal conduct sheet. I knew that my conviction would prevent this. But what should I do now that my conviction was quashed? There were four years left on my contract and I didn't want to jeopardise my hard-earned pension.

I was approached by some Royal Army Medical Corps (RAMC) officers who were based at 3 Division. They had been watching me and liked how I got things done. Why didn't I apply to become a commissioned officer with their regiment?

The RAMC appealed to me. It offered a different role after my experiences as a front-line warrior. I was especially impressed with their CO, Colonel Kevin Beaton, who had flown to Iraq with me in 2003 and had been the first doctor to treat Tommo. The RAMC was less snobbish and narrow-minded than the Black Watch. My old regiment had never appointed a Catholic RSM and you had to ask the CO's permission to get married – living with a girlfriend was frowned upon. At the same time, I wasn't happy with the plan to merge the Black Watch into a new Scottish super-regiment. And, crucially, I couldn't stomach the thought of returning to the institution that had shafted me after two decades' loyal service.

Eventually, I handed in my commissioning application to the RAMC. I wasn't hopeful: 290 people were competing for 7 places and I was an outsider. It was a lengthy process of form filling and interviews with senior officers. My first was with a colonel who was the chief medical officer at 3 Division. Inevitably, we spoke about my conviction and successful appeal. 'I think it is commendable that you took the stand that you did,' he said. 'Commander's head off and doctor's head on: how has all this affected you as an individual?' I felt my bottom lip quiver despite myself as I explained a little about my continued anguish. He listened sympathetically and I passed through to the next round – and then all the way to a final interview with the commissioning board, a panel of colonels and brigadiers.

I faced a stream of questions. What sort of man was I? What sort of person makes a good officer? What management skills are needed? What is the difference between an officer and a soldier? They did the 'good cop, bad cop' routine and I tried to sell myself without overdoing it. My quashed conviction was just touched upon; it was in the past, they said.

Just before Christmas, I learned that I'd made it. I had a choice of commissions and felt honoured when Kevin Beaton called and asked me to be his quartermaster. On 1 April 2005, I became Captain Tam Henderson, the youngest quartermaster in the British Army.

In January 2005, Julie gave birth to our daughter Holly, who is beautiful and full of fun. We were a family now and I felt apprehensive when I heard the news of my next posting. I was going back to Iraq for five months.

• • •

In June 2005, at Basra airport, I put down my bag and almost keeled over as the memories from 2003 flooded back. I was delighted when Kevin arrived in person to drive me to my base at Shaibah.

Then, the next morning, he asked to see me. 'This is the RAMC Powerpoint presentation we show to visitors,' he said, flicking through a series of slides. Suddenly, I was looking at photos of Tommo, who, Kevin explained, had assisted the regiment's training by taking part in realistic scenarios in which the medics dealt with casualties who had lost limbs.

'Would you like to see some pictures of his injuries?' Kevin asked. I felt overwhelmed seeing photos of Tommo taken immediately after the chain gun shot him. He had suffered terribly and was very lucky to be alive.

As I walked around the Shaibah airbase, I suddenly saw Talib, our Mr Fix-It from the last tour. He fell to his knees. 'Meester Tam, how are you? I did not expect to see you again.' Talib had run a little stall for the Jocks at Camp Stephen, selling handy stuff like razors and batteries. Now he ran a shop at Shaibah with his brother, who had been one of my interpreters. He was doing OK, unlike most of my former staff from Camp Stephen. Wahlid, my chief interpreter and friend, had been shot dead when he returned to work at the university. Several more of my interpreters had been killed and others had fled to Jordan. I felt guilty and angry that many of the Iraqis who had risked their lives supporting us had suffered.

My arrival coincided with the appearance of new, deadly, precision-made mines. These were being smuggled in from Iran. Insurgents used the devices to fire armour-piercing explosively formed projectiles, or EFPs, directly into armoured vehicles. Our death and injury tolls mounted.

As quartermaster, I was responsible for all the equipment – from needles to CT scanners – at the 175-bed Shaibah military hospital, which handled casualties across southern Iraq. I also equipped our 340 medics, who were infantry trained and went out on dangerous missions. Soon, I was drawn into a war of words with the authorities over shortages and shoddy gear.

I was stunned to discover that the medics were protecting ambulances with nothing but old-fashioned iron sights on their rifles. They were the only British unit in Iraq not supplied with up-to-date SUSAT rifle sights with times-four magnification, laser-module night-sights and the helmet-mounted night-vision sights (HMNVS) that we had used in 2003 to see in the dark and frighten potential enemies by placing laser dots on their chests.

The army issued instructions for dealing with the growing EFP threat. These told us to use the magnification on our SUSATs to try to identify the devices. But what were the medics supposed to do? I made a huge fuss, which culminated in a showdown with the heads of logistics, including a colonel.

As far as I was concerned, the people in charge were bean counters who didn't understand that the medics had a fighting role and needed to protect themselves and any casualties they were carrying back to hospital. I spoke about my own experiences, about how I had used the night-sights to survive. 'If anyone dies as a result of this negligence,' I told them, 'I will tell the investigating officers that you refused my request.' The equipment was soon found and the medics were trained to use it. Then the army issued an instruction that every soldier in Iraq must be issued with a SUSAT.

I had less success with our helmets. The Mark 6A model was a big improvement on the Mark 6. Reinforced with Kevlar – five times stronger than steel – it boosted your chances of surviving an EFP. But we only had 100 of these helmets and most of the medics had to use the flimsier ones, which wasn't good for morale.

The use of Snatch Land Rovers was another scandal. These armoured vehicles offered little protection from explosions and were top-heavy and liable to topple over when turning corners at speed. Several soldiers have been killed and injured while travelling in them and the Government took too long to accept responsibility for the risks involved and take action.

There were many deficiencies in the hospital, too. When a consultant decided to use an out-of-date drug to try to save the life of a soldier from the Royal Irish Regiment, his gamble paid off but sparked an investigation. I was horrified to discover that companies were offloading drugs approaching their sell-by date to us because the NHS wouldn't take them. There was a shortage of titanium leg braces for soldiers seriously wounded by EFPs. It is probable that men lost their legs because of this. We even ran out of coffins. I was deeply ashamed when we had to return four dead US marines to their regiment in body-bags. We started borrowing coffins from the Americans until new supplies arrived and even then we didn't have the right range of sizes.

During that second tour, Major Simon Powell, the RAMC second in command, handed me a copy of the Munitions Incident Report for 2004. 'Have a look at this,' he said, pointing to a page. I felt blind rage reading that an Iraqi man had been killed and a woman injured in Basra as a result of an undemanded firing by a Warrior chain gun. Despite my court case, nothing had been done to fix the faults. How many more innocent people had to be killed and maimed before changes were made?

The shortages and problems with equipment were a catalogue of shame, showing how little the Government cared about us. While

I was in Iraq, I met Lieutenant Colonel Nick Henderson, the CO of the Coldstream Guards. He lost four of his men during a six-month tour of duty. On his return home, he resigned in protest at the lack of resources.

It seemed to me during this second tour that we had lost our grip on Basra. Shia militias had thoroughly infiltrated the police. This was clearly demonstrated in September 2005 when two SAS guys were arrested at a checkpoint, taken to the al-Jamariah police station (where I had confronted rioters two years before) and handed over to militiamen. Fortunately, a US spy plane spotted where they were taken. When a party of Brits went unarmed to negotiate with the police, they were thrown into jail. Warriors were then sent to rescue the SAS men; they smashed down a wall of Basra prison to release our negotiators. Meanwhile, a hostile crowd had gathered, and Sergeant George Long and Private Ryon Burton leaped in flames from their Warrior when it was petrol bombed by rioters. I met them at the hospital, badly burned but alive.

I spoke to a US marine commander who had lost men when their Humvee was bombed. He was in tears as I explained that, having been in combat, I truly knew how he felt.

'How do I deal with my men who survived?' he asked.

'There could be a lot of guilt and blame,' I said. 'It's inevitable after the trauma. They need you to encourage them to talk their feelings through.'

Another time, four critically injured interpreters working with the Americans were brought to Shaibah. Three Jordanians were transferred to intensive care at a US military hospital in the Green Zone. The fourth interpreter was denied access to those facilities because he was an Iraqi national. The Jordanians survived and he died.

We treated several Iraqi insurgents at Shaibah. One guy had been injured by his own bomb. He told me that he had worked for the Americans as an interpreter but had been offered much more money to blow them up. Others were badly wounded after firefights with our guys. I looked at them and thought, once more, what would I be doing in their circumstances?

I spoke to many British Army patients and all of them were unhappy about the war. Why are we here, they asked? What have I lost my leg for? One of my Warrior crew from 2003 came for psychiatric treatment. I walked around the hospital grounds with him. 'I want to go home,' he said. So did I.

TWENTY-ONE

Dulce et Decorum Est

After almost six months away, I returned to our new home, near Catterick army base in North Yorkshire, looking forward to a family Christmas. Then Captain Chris Gibson, the operations officer for the 3 Close Support Regiment, called me. 'We need you to join a humanitarian reconnaissance mission in Kenya in January,' he said. At least I would spend Christmas at home. However, it would mean missing Holly's first birthday. Julie was supportive but she had recently left the army to look after our baby and I was thinking hard about my own future.

We landed at Nairobi airport, under the gaze of giraffes in the nearby national park, and drove past five-star hotels and slums to BATUK (British Army Training Unit Kenya) on the outskirts of the city. With Colonel Kevin Beaton and the rest of our team, I was briefed about the operation by 'Red Angus', whom I knew from the Black Watch. We were going north, on a long journey to a village called Loiyangalani, near Lake Turkana. We were investigating the feasibility of setting up an army medical station there. It was a humanitarian mission but it was clear that there was also an intelligence-gathering agenda. Al-Qaeda was active on the Somali border further north and in 1998 it had bombed the US Embassy in Nairobi, slaughtering hundreds of Kenyans and Americans. We were advised that al-Qaeda had undertaken bombing preparations in the area near Loiyangalani and we were told to watch out for the *shiftas* – the local bandits.

At first, we passed through lush country, teeming with wildlife. On a three-hour drive, I spotted elephants, giraffes, boars, water buffalo, gazelles, jackals and cheetahs. We stopped for the night at the British Army base in Nanyuki. Then, on the next day's journey, we seemed to step back in time. There were no more tarmac roads, just rough dust tracks that punctured our tyres and forced me to don my Iraqi wear – a shemagh and huge goggles. Suddenly, we were in an arid desert. Then we slowly climbed a range of extinct volcanoes before stopping at Marsabit, a small town surrounded by forest. In the morning, we made a perilous descent through a pockmarked lunar landscape, littered with ash and the bones of creatures that had died in the droughts.

At last, we reached new plains and drove on to Loiyangalani, which means 'a place of many trees'. The village was founded in the 1960s, near a freshwater spring, and draws together three tribes: the Turkana, Elmolo and Samburu. The Turkana men looked like Mohicans to me, sporting distinctive loincloths and with one side of their heads shaven. Their women wore lots of necklaces and many carried mirrors to check their dyed-red hair. One guy introduced himself to me as 'Night Warrior' because he carried a torch. That first evening, I went to a village dance. With the men's dramatic posturing and the women's beautiful song, it was a mesmerising performance.

In Loiyangalani, I also visited two families of American missionaries. 'They're the CIA,' joked a German who ran a local tourist hostel. But I quickly warmed to Cheryl and Tim and Barbara and Jim. They had come to the town 15 years previously, when their children were toddlers, and had lived in mud huts until they had built their own houses. They preached the Bible but also provided practical help to the locals, using their basic medical skills and helping to build a three-mile pipe bringing fresh water into town.

'Will you help us with our mission?' I asked them. 'We want to bring a big team of medics here for a couple of months to carry out an inoculation programme and distribute mosquito nets.'

'Of course,' said Jim, without hesitation. 'We'll do whatever we can to assist you.'

We spent several days scouting the area, led by Tim and Jim, who knew the dangers from animals and shiftas. They carried G3 long-barrelled rifles and 9-mm pistols. They also had military-style quad bikes, which we used to recce for outposts from where our medics could deliver aid. Our big concern was that the civil conflict in Somalia was spilling over the border. I had to balance giving local tribespeople access to medical help with keeping my men safe.

One day, we stopped for water at the northern edge of Lake Turkana and, through my binoculars, I watched three Elmolo men fishing with nets. All of a sudden, two crocodiles popped up behind them. I held my breath but the men turned and tossed fish to the reptiles, which then, astonishingly, disappeared.

Back in England, we practised transporting 200 men and vital equipment through hazardous terrain, travelling from Salisbury Plain up to Catterick Garrison. North of Marsabit, we wouldn't be able to drive anything bigger than a Land Rover. We would also need mobile fridges to keep the medicines at a constant temperature.

In May, I returned to Kenya for two months to prepare three aid centres: one at Nanyuki, another at Marsabit and the third, with the help of my missionary friends, at Loiyangalani. In Nanyuki, we had the support of a British army base; further north, we were on our own. As the quartermaster, I had to ensure that 200 troops could survive the rigours of life in the bush for more than a month. For some, this would be the biggest test of their lives. Much of Kenya had been gripped by a long drought and water was vital to our success. I drew on my experiences of setting up Camp Stephen. Each centre would have a tented HQ and armed medical patrols would deploy from these to remote outstations so that we would get aid out to where it was most needed.

In Nairobi, I met our medics, a surgical field team, a dental field team and combat medics. We took 30 vehicles and trailers through desert, swamps and rivers and along slender cliff paths. Our drivers wondered if we could make it but I'd done it before and pushed them on. We were carrying durable silk 'escape and evasion' maps. At one point, we came under fire from shiftas armed with AK-47s but they melted away when we stopped and dismounted.

The mission went well. We gave life-saving vaccinations to 10,000 people, mosquito nets to 5,000 women and children, and, in a dental hygiene blitz, extracted 1,000 teeth.

Back in Nairobi, Kevin and I went for dinner with an SAS colonel who showed a keen interest in our experiences and especially in the movements of the shiftas. Then two generals visited us: General Sheriff, the 3 (UK) Divisional commander, and General Hawley, the commander of the Army Medical Services. They were battle-hardened, two of the most respected generals in the army. I drove them all the way to Loiyangalani. General Sheriff was born in Kenya – his father was a district commissioner – and we stopped at his old house on the journey.

They were impressed by our achievements. 'It's a huge success,' said General Sheriff. 'And you've done a great job getting all these men and their equipment here safely.'

'But tell me,' he continued. 'How do you feel about doing this kind of work after all your experience? Don't you want to be back in a combat role?'

I handed them a couple of photographs. They showed a local man with his daughter, who was about two. In one, the father was in despair because his child, bitten by a puff adder and with her face badly swollen, seemed doomed to die. In the second, the man looked overjoyed because the girl had been given anti-venom and would survive. I was part of the emergency support operation that flew in a doctor with the antidote that saved her life. It's hard to describe the huge impact that this had on me. I could have been that father and the girl could have been my Holly.

'I have spent twenty years in the infantry, planning and executing the taking of life,' I told the generals, 'and two years with the Royal Army Medical Corps planning and executing the saving of life.

Those two years have been the most challenging and satisfying. Taking life is not difficult. Saving and sustaining life is. It has given me the greatest satisfaction being a part of this mission.'

I knew that my army life was over. Something fundamental had changed in me. I was glad to finish my career by doing good.

• • •

My most recent army reports had said that I should set my sights on becoming a colonel. But I knew it was time to go. In spirit, I had already left the army, on 20 June 2003, the day when I was sent home from Basra in disgrace. To me, everything that had happened since then was an epilogue. Even my successful appeal didn't truly feel like a victory. It couldn't compensate for my deep hurt and disappointment. I had given everything to the Black Watch and the army but they had turned around and said: 'You are not that important to us.'

I saw my own betrayal as symbolic of that felt by so many British soldiers who served in Iraq. In 2000, the unspoken pact between society and the military was formally codified in the Military Covenant. This states:

> Soldiers will be called upon to make personal sacrifices – including the ultimate sacrifice – in the service of the nation. In putting the needs of the nation and the army before their own, they forgo some of the rights enjoyed by those outside the armed forces. In return, British soldiers must always be able to expect fair treatment, to be valued and respected as individuals and that they (and their families) will be sustained and rewarded by commensurate terms and conditions of service.

Just three years later, the Government reneged on this agreement by its treatment of British troops fighting in Iraq. Soldiers were killed and maimed because they didn't have the right kit and were given shoddy gear like the chain gun. In 2005, as a quartermaster,

I saw that troops were still being denied life-saving equipment.

Even our accommodation at Shaibah – two years after the invasion – was a disgrace. We soldiers slept in aluminium Portakabins, while the UN police at our camp had concrete-reinforced ones. In a mortar attack, we would likely die and they would likely live. They were in a union and had quite rightly demanded more protection.

Warren Lister, the expert witness at my appeal, estimated that it would cost about £16 million to remedy the flaws on the chain gun. This is a drop in the ocean in comparison with the £6 billion spent so far by the British government on the war. Yet nothing has been done, even though the Ministry of Defence has itself reported that the fault killed at least one innocent person after Tommo's accident.

I was pleased that Tommo eventually got substantial compensation from the MoD – but initially they refused to pay him a penny. It took the threat of a court case following my appeal to make them cough up.

Our soldiers have not had enough help in dealing with the mental wounds of war. A scab forms eventually but it can easily reopen if the underlying sore isn't dealt with. When you have killed, nearly been killed or seen your comrades killed, you are vulnerable to every associated image, news report and film clip. Just driving down a motorway, I notice army trucks and wonder, 'Where have they been? Where are they going?' And then the dark memories flood back. I know several brave men who have suffered from depression, post-traumatic stress disorder or 'war shock' – call it what you will. In this context, talk of a stiff upper lip is utter bollocks.

And what was it all for? I will forever carry the guilt of having taken people's lives. I welcomed the war as my greatest career challenge after 20 years' training. But I also believed the Government's claim that this was a just conflict to make Britain safer and to defeat tyranny. Now I feel that I was fighting for a lie. There were no weapons of mass destruction, not even in a little green box beneath a Basra steel factory. Saddam Hussein posed no threat to us whatsoever. I can't say if it was a war for oil but what I did see was plenty of American and British firms arriving with huge contracts for rebuilding Iraq's bombed infrastructure.

Al-Qaeda went into Iraq *after* we invaded it. We helped by creating an excellent training ground for terrorists. Britain now faces a bigger terrorist threat than ever before. This scares me. I no longer have a gun, helmet and body armour to protect me – not that they would be much use against an anonymous suicide bomber. Since 2003, hundreds of thousands of Iraqis have died violently and the conflict is seemingly endless. Before the invasion, most Iraqi women went freely about their business. Since it, there has been a sharp rise in honour killings as a result of a combination of political instability and growing religious conservatism. It is not a legacy to be proud of.

Back at home, the Government has shamefully tried to gag coroners reporting on inquests into the deaths of British soldiers killed on active service, taking court action in an attempt to prevent them from criticising the MoD. Bereaved mums and dads have the right to know the coroner's true opinion of the reason for a son's or daughter's death. What's more, the public outcry following critical coroners' reports has sometimes saved soldiers' lives. In 2005, for example, it led to the issuing of the more effective (and expensive) Osprey body armour.

I fully support calls for a public inquiry into all aspects of the Iraq War. It could generate lasting improvements in soldiers' conditions, just as the Franks Inquiry into the Falklands War led to the issuing of better boots to prevent trench-foot. The whole truth about the Iraq War needs to be laid bare.

Our soldiers are still dying out there for no good reason. In April 2007 – my last month in the army – eleven members of my garrison were killed. They included two members of my regiment, one a young woman of nineteen. I helped with their funeral arrangements; I have helped to bury far too many people during the last five years.

In Afghanistan, too, we are fighting a war we cannot win, with one major result being that Britain's streets have been flooded with cheap heroin. It is high time the troops were brought home.

I have not become a pacifist. We need an army that is ready to defend the country. But, in my view, the only other circumstance in which it should be deployed is as an unequivocal force for good, providing robust support for humanitarian missions. And at all times, our soldiers must be given the respect promised them in the Military Covenant and the best equipment available.

• • •

Do I regret joining the army? My answer is a clear no. Through the Black Watch, I forged my identity as a young man and gained a sense of belonging. My final quarrel was with the high command and not with the men of the Black Watch. The army gave me self-esteem and a specialised but invaluable education. From the age of 16, I learned to be a leader and became imbued with values such as honour and respect. I also loved the rigorous training and learning new skills. I remember a briefing for the army's adventure training programme that said it was designed to 'enhance leadership skills, build team work and push the boundaries of individual courage'.

That programme also gave birth to my enduring passion: diving. This began quite accidentally in the mid-'90s at the Magilligan Training Centre in Northern Ireland. Faced with a £78 bill to renew my Parachute Association membership, I opted instead to pay £13 to go diving, even though I wasn't the strongest swimmer. The moment a wee crab swam past me, I was hooked. I went on to become a nationally qualified instructor and the diving officer at Sandhurst. We took a team to the Red Sea, where we visited the haunting Second World War wreck of the SS *Thistlegorm*. Diving lets you explore another fascinating world.

Today, I do miss the comradeship of army life and wish civvy street was less uncaring. Despite Iraq, there were many more highs than lows for me in my army career. The boy of 16 who joined up has gone for ever, in some ways for the good, in others for the bad. But the balance is positive. My world now is full of new challenges, including running our restaurant business and diving centre on the Isle of Skye. I will work hard for my family's happiness. Life is good.